STANDING FOR CHRIST
IN A MODERN BABYLON

OTHER BOOKS BY MARVIN OLASKY

ON FIGHTING POVERTY

Compassionate Conservatism:
What It Is, What It Does, and How It Can Transform America

Renewing American Compassion:
How Compassion for the Needy Can Turn Ordinary Citizens into Heroes

The Tragedy of American Compassion

Patterns of Corporate Philanthropy

More Than Kindness (with Susan Olasky)

ON AMERICAN HISTORY

The American Leadership Tradition:
Moral Vision from Washington to Clinton

Fighting for Liberty and Virtue:
Political and Cultural Wars in Eighteenth-Century America

Philanthropically Correct: The Story of the Council on Foundations

Abortion Rites: A Social History of Abortion in America

Corporate Public Relations: A New Historical Perspective

ON JOURNALISM

Telling the Truth: How to Revitalize Christian Journalism

Central Ideas in the Development of American Journalism

The Press and Abortion, 1838-1988

Prodigal Press: The Anti-Christian Bias of the American News Media

Whirled Views (with Joel Belz)

STANDING FOR CHRIST IN A MODERN BABYLON

Marvin Olasky

CROSSWAY BOOKS

A DIVISION OF
GOOD NEWS PUBLISHERS
WHEATON, ILLINOIS

Library of Congress Cataloging-in-Publication Data
Olasky, Marvin N.
  Standing for Christ in a modern Babylon / Marvin Olasky.
    p. cm.
  Includes bibliographical references.
  ISBN 1-58134-474-0 (tpb. : alk. paper)
  1. Christianity and culture—United States. 2. Religion and the press—United States. 3. United States—Moral conditions. I. Title.
BR517.O43   2003
261'.0973—dc21   2002154720

ML		13	12	11	10	09	08	07	06	05	04	03
15	14	13	12	11	10	9	8	7	6	5	4	3	2	1

To
NICK EICHER, JOEL BELZ, BOB JONES,
MINDY BELZ, ED VEITH, LYNN VINCENT,
TIM LAMER, DAVID FREELAND
and other colleagues at *World*
who stand for Christ in a very exposed way.

TABLE OF CONTENTS

INTRODUCTION

The modern battle to preserve civilization and recognize its religious source began on September 11, 2001. When the second terrorist airplane attacked the World Trade Center, ABC's Diane Sawyer was speechless for a moment. Then she uttered a soft, "Oh, my God."

As the first of the twin towers collapsed, pastoral staff members at Trinity Church Wall Street were leading prayers and hymns. Dust penetrated Trinity's office tower and filled the lobby as congregants evacuated children from the basement pre-school, and then fled screaming onto Broadway. The church could not stay separate from the sins of the world.

As excavation crews worked at the Manhattan death site, mourners and passers-by stuck prayers on fences and walls. "Lord Jesus Christ," read one, "have mercy on us. Make haste to help us. Comfort us. Rescue us. And save us. Do your will in our lives." President George W. Bush quoted from Psalm 23 and emphasized prayer in his speeches to the nation. For several months the United States was in a foxhole, and atheistic assumptions were under fire.

A year later, though, other catastrophic terrorist attacks had not occurred; so many Americans filed away larger questions, and many journalists returned to snide attacks on those who offered answers. Meanwhile, many conservative Christians maintained a posture of just saying no to modern and postmodern craziness, instead of engaging American culture and developing alternatives.

That great divide could be especially tragic given what happened in the rest of the world during 2002 as America returned, perhaps temporarily, to pre-September 11 normality. One example: In mid-November, 2002, Nigerian Muslim anger over a newspaper article about the Miss World beauty pageant touched off riots that left 220 persons dead and over 1,000 seriously injured, along with numerous Christian churches burned to the ground.

How bad was it? *Los Angeles Times* correspondent Davan Maharaj reported that "Thousands of Muslim youths armed with knives and machetes [were] burning cars and assaulting bystanders they suspected were Christian. Rioters pulled a local journalist off a motorcycle and told him he would be killed unless he could recite verses from Islam's holy book, the Quran. The crowd released him unharmed when they realized he was Muslim."

The article in the Nigerian newspaper *ThisDay* speculated that Muhammad, instead of reacting like the contemporary opponents of the beauty pageants, "would have probably chosen a wife" from among the contestants. Given the tinder box that Islamic extremists have made of northern Nigeria, the comment was dumb—but it was also a reasonable speculation, for stories about Muhammad's life that have semi-sacred status within Islam show the religion's founder appreciating and sometimes appropriating to himself the beauties of his time.

Book eight, numbers 3325 and 3328, of the sayings and deeds collected by the esteemed ninth-century editor Abul Husain Muslim bin al-Hajjaj al-Nisapuri records how Muhammad heard that a young woman was so beautiful that a disciple said, "she is worthy of you only." Muhammad had her brought to him and was so enraptured that he "granted her emancipation and married her."

ThisDay could have footnoted its story with these and other references—but that would have increased the tensions. Nigeria's Islamic extremists don't want anyone to raise questions about how Muhammad actually lived, because that might hurt their effort to set up an autocratic Islamic regime. Some countries under Christian influence were like that centuries ago, but they eventually adopted the view John Milton expressed in the 1640s in his *Areopagetica*. Milton wrote, "Though all the winds of doctrine were let loose to play upon the earth, so truth be in the field . . . let her and falsehood grapple; who ever knew truth put to the worse, in a free and open encounter."

Milton's prescription is still suspect in much of the world. Nigerian President Olusegun Obasanjo criticized *ThisDay* and said murderous riots could happen in his country "any time irresponsible journalism is committed against Islam." That's what is so sad: This is not a one-time occurrence but something to be expected "any time." The enemies of journalistic freedom used to have their capital in Moscow; now it's Mecca. Hardcore Islam has now replaced communism as the world's most potent hater of press liberty.

Christians, confident of God's providence, should defend Milton's view—but sometimes we don't. My concern about missed opportunities engendered this book, which briefly reports and analyzes where American culture now stands, with an emphasis on the chasm between secular liberal journalists and conservative Christians. This book deals with how Christians should act and talk within a culture that's both liberal and libertine. It shows how Christians need to exercise discernment in proposing addition, not subtraction: Unable to eliminate wrongful choices, we need to add godly ones.

This book also shows how Christians can respond to typical press attacks in a way that can not only win points but point journalists to Him. Some people who would like to stand for Christ become irate, even despairing, but the Bible shows how believers have been a harassed minority before, and under much more difficult circumstances than those we now face. The last chapter of 2 Chronicles tells the 2,600-year-old saga: The Babylonians "burned the house of God and broke down the wall of Jerusalem and burned all its palaces with fire and destroyed all its precious vessels" (2 Chron. 36:19 ESV).

Israelites had lived in a land where every aspect of life was to point them to the holiness of the one God who reigned above all. Suddenly, they found themselves exiled to Babylon. They found there a land of many gods where almost anything was allowed as long as it did not interfere with obeying and paying tribute to the king. Some Israelites probably sequestered themselves as much as they could from Babylonian civilization. The Old Testament tells of Daniel and a few other young men enrolling in a three-year course in Babylon designed to leave them with an M.B.A.—Master of Babylonian Arts.

Daniel, after graduation, came to prominence when God gave him the grace to comprehend and interpret a dream of King Nebuchadnezzar. Providentially, Daniel had gained the understanding of Babylonian culture that he needed to communicate powerfully the essence of the dream. He told the king of a great image with a head of gold, chest and arms of silver, middle and thighs of bronze, legs of iron, and feet partly of iron and partly of clay. All of these aspects had meanings that Daniel laid out, but the climax of the dream and interpretation came when a stone cut from a mountain by no human hand broke the statue into pieces, and that stone then "became a great mountain and filled the whole earth" (Dan. 2:35 ESV).

Daniel, knowing how Babylonians saw mountains either as gods or the abode of gods, then explained that the powerful stone came from not a mere mountain god but from ". . . the God of heaven [who] will set up a kingdom that shall never be destroyed" (v. 44 ESV). Nebuchadnezzar realized that Daniel's knowledge of the dream could have come about only through a god's doing. He also gained a vision of the mightiness of this God and told Daniel, "Truly your God is God of gods and Lord of kings . . ." (v. 47 ESV).

Nebuchadnezzar made Daniel ruler over the central part of the Babylonian empire, and the Israelite in succeeding decades was in and out of the Babylonian court. He spoke forthrightly to Nebuchadnezzar by telling his patron that he would become insane for seven years.

Daniel was forgotten by a second king but brought back just in time to predict the kingdom's imminent fall. Daniel did not go looking for trouble, but trouble came looking for him: Praying in his own home, he ended up thrown to the lions. God then delivered Daniel and so impressed a third king, Darius, that the monarch recognized "the God of Daniel" as "the living God, enduring forever" (Dan. 6:26 ESV).

Daniel, faithful to biblical understanding but comprehending Babylon, is a role model for Christians who want to work in the dominant culture of America but not be of it. Daniel's life was not easy— at least twice it almost ended prematurely—and he spent his entire career among people of different beliefs. But he stood for God decade after decade, and we can do the same. He had to be bilingual and bicultural, and so should we be.

We know that not only from the example of Daniel, but also from God's command. The prophet Jeremiah wrote, "Thus says the LORD of hosts, the God of Israel, to all the exiles whom I have sent into exile from Jerusalem to Babylon: 'Build houses and live in them; plant gardens and eat their produce. . . . Seek the welfare of the city where I have sent you into exile, and pray to the LORD on its behalf, for in its welfare you will find your welfare'" (29:4-7 ESV). In the last book of the Bible, Revelation, "Babylon" is the symbol of everything wicked, but that's not how Jeremiah refers to it. In his day Babylonia was a mighty civilization that generally tolerated many minority religions, including worship of the true God. Many Babylonians were good neighbors, trading gardening tips.

Today biblical Christians should see fellow citizens in America not as enemies but as needy people. This book can help Christians rooted in one culture to communicate with neighbors in another. It is designed to help Christians stand up resolutely against press attacks and to see them as opportunities to communicate the truth about false religions and about Christianity. It is secondarily intended to help us look in the mirror and see ourselves as secular liberal journalists often see us. Our goal should be to minimize unnecessary press criticism while maximizing a Christian witness that should lead to even more criticism—but the right kind.

The first chapter emphasizes the importance of understanding "choice" as a god-word in America, and proposes that Christians, instead of looking for ways to escape our liberty theme park, follow the advice of Booker T. Washington: "Throw down your bucket where you are." It examines the meanings of freedom and liberty and their historical connection to family and love. It proposes a pro-life strategy of doubling the choices women have and emphasizes the importance of positioning Christianity as pro-choice (including giving unborn children a chance), diverse, pragmatic, skeptical, patient, optimistic, and content—but never passive.

The second chapter suggests that we should listen to the critiques secularists offer because some may be like those Shimei hurled at King David 3,000 years ago. David would not let his soldiers kill the dirt-thrower because he just might be a helpful messenger. Non-biblical restrictions on conduct, along with anti-biblical racial bias, have hurt the church's witness, and we should admit those failings and others. The chapter lays out a "rapids test" that can help us be strict constructionists regarding Scripture. Then comes a critique of the attacks leveled at Christians since September 11, 2001, by the *New York Times*, the *Washington Post*, and other publications, and an assessment of whether these attacks are the result of ignorance, malice, or Christophobia.

Chapter 3 examines the ignorance that many secularists have about Christianity's societal impact. Sneering scorn needs to be fought with recognition of emotion but also a recital of facts about the worldwide spread of Christianity, the role of Christians in American history and politics over the past two centuries, and the long-lived Christian interaction with government. Journalists need to hear the stories of well-known athletes like Kurt Warner and John Smoltz and little-known compassionate crusaders in poor areas of major cities. We should avoid covering up Christian failings but should also show that those who are needy at home and abroad will lose a major source of help if reporters further marginalize Christians.

Chapter 4 shows how the search for greener grass elsewhere has led some journalists to praise Eastern religions and several ideologies that spoke of freedom but gave us gulags—and how journalists, fearful of seeming anti-Muslim, are playing a role in a new bait-and-switch game. The chapter notes that many Muslims are good neighbors in the United States, but that for over 1,300 years Islamic rule has dropped non-Muslims into "dhimmitude," a state in many ways worse than servitude. Press inaccuracy about Christianity is matched by inaccurate depictions of Islam that currently pervade American media and may lead us to fatal distraction.

Chapter 5 outlines points of contact with secularists that will help Christians meet our prime obligation: not defending ourselves against attack but proclaiming boldly and winsomely the gospel of grace. Although we are not to be quarrelsome, and we should turn the other cheek concerning personal offenses, we must be ready to debate when basic biblical principles are at stake. When people whisper, "Did God really say . . ." as the serpent insinuated in Eden, we need to say, "Yes, He did." When people want us to go with the flow, to meet "halfway," we need to stand our ground whenever it is good ground, high ground, God's ground.

That will cost us, but the willingness to forgo applause from society's trendsetters distinguishes tough Christians from the Mr. Pliables of the world. We can be confident that our focus is biblical when we answer correctly the party game question: If you could have any dinner guest you wanted, whom would you invite? Lots of guests would be entertaining. Some would offer instruction. But only one would change not just some things but everything in the lives of those at the dinner table. If the resurrected Jesus came for a fish fry, showing His punctured palms and wounded side, that would make all the difference for guests with eyes to see and ears to hear Him.

Christians who understand their societies and become God's

instruments can make a huge difference for individuals and whole cultures. As this book shows, we can fight pornography not with talk of eradicating filth but with a call to preserve individual rights, including the right not to have porn shoved into our e-mail or popping up as we web-surf. We can defend the Boy Scout ban on homosexual scoutmasters as a recognition of consumer choice and the rights of the poor: How many single moms, enrolling their sons in the Boy Scouts so they will have male role models, want them to be mentored by gay men?

This book is about how to talk with our neighbors in this modern Babylon about such issues and others, both domestic and international. If we think living in Babylon is too hard, we can remember the experience of Daniel and many others. We can also come to understand that the question about which dinner guest to invite is in one sense irrelevant. Jesus doesn't wait for invitations. Whenever He chooses to come, He crashes the party. That can always give us hope.

LIVING IN THE
LIBERTY THEME PARK

Christians often fall into traps. The perpetrators and venues change: In 1990, Mapplethorpe in Cincinnati; in 1999, Ofili in Brooklyn; in 2002, the University of North Carolina. The common denominator: Religious protesters, attacking profane artistic presentations and biased academic endeavors, walked into a journalistic snare.

The repeated ploy of the cultural left is to put forth a "work of art" calculated to outrage conservative evangelicals and traditional Catholics, who respond as if on cue by demanding that the outrage be removed. Typical incitement: The October 2, 1999, opening of an exhibition at the Brooklyn Museum of Art that featured a dung-and-pornography-bedecked painting of "The Holy Virgin Mary." Typical reaction: a demonstration by 200 Catholic League supporters. Associated Press coverage: "One grim-faced man brandished a sign that read, 'Hitler Was Right When He Got Rid of Degenerate Art.'"

A different theme could have emerged from this face-off. Rudy Giuliani, then mayor of New York and two years from gaining broad respect during the weeks after the 9/11 attacks, asked why taxpayers should subsidize the profane tastes of a few. But the *New York Times* played down that question and played up the "Hitler Was Right" sign. Its front-page story juxtaposed the record number of attendees at the opening (9,200) with the arrival of a "busload of women" from a

Catholic church who described themselves as "soldiers of Mary . . . come to her defense."

The *Times* reporter on October 3 did quote one protester saying, "The issue is the funding," but that statement was overshadowed by a full paragraph about how a man with a loudspeaker kept reciting the rosary. The reporter was careful to note that the protester "did this for hours, so much so that some people leaving the exhibition mockingly parroted the prayer as they headed for their cars." Articles in other newspapers that week criticized that one religious group for purportedly trying to impose its morals on the general populace.

That is something no one can stare down these days in our laid-back culture. The result was obvious as soon as pundits successfully categorized the battle as liberty versus repression. Readers could cheer a victory for artistic freedom and the liberty of individuals to choose to go to a controversial exhibit. Readers could boo religious bigots and their attempt to take away choices from individuals.

Nearly three years later, when the University of North Carolina required incoming freshmen to read portions of the Quran (embedded in a favorable commentary, with portions that justify killing opponents omitted), a Christian group demanded that the book be removed from reading lists. That action was logical according to the First Amendment. Government officials are not supposed to give official preference to one religion over another, but foolish according to today's last amendment: Journalists get the last word.

It would have been far better to ask not that a book be removed, but that portions of the Bible be added to the reading list. In our touchy society less cannot be more; it is better ethically to give rather than receive, but it is essential politically to add rather than subtract. Whenever media powers frame the issue as "repression" or "censorship," Christians and conservatives lose. We can whine about dumbness and unfairness, but we need a new strategy, one based on the understanding that modern America and ancient Israel are two very different places.

Ancient Israel, to use today's parlance, was a holiness theme park. The laws laid down by Moses set up Israel to be a holy people separated from others and dedicated to God. The land itself was a theme park with everything—geography, economics, laws, customs—stressing holiness. In the end, of course, the insufficiency of all those aids to reverence showed man's desperate need for Christ.

The United States, though, is a theme park devoted to liberty. We are the envy of much of the world because of the freedom we have to speak, write, worship, and work. We are free to build businesses and to travel. We are also free to consume pornography, practice adultery and homosexuality, and act in other ways that threaten life and the pursuit of long-term happiness, because a lesson regularly taught in the eighteenth century has now largely been forgotten: Liberty without virtue becomes license, and licentiousness leads to anarchy.

THE HISTORICAL MEANING OF FREEDOM AND LIBERTY

Journalists I've talked with sometimes think of God as a cruel dictator, but that shows a misunderstanding of both human nature and the meaning of freedom. To grasp this we need to go on a brief etymological excursion, tracing the word *freedom* to its German origins. Today, watching beer commercials in America or Germany, we might suspect that freedom means to be unencumbered by family, completely at liberty to satisfy any desires at any time with anyone. But the word *free* in Old High German, as Gregory Beabout of Saint Louis University has noted, stems from the Indo-European *prijos* (dear, beloved) and is related to the Sanskrit *priyas* (dear) and *priya* (wife, daughter).

The word *free* is also connected to the Old English *frigu* (love); Germans and Celts used it to mean neither controlled from outside the household nor enslaved, but benevolent toward and intimate with those inside. In Danish, *frie* means "to make an offer of marriage," which should be done both through free choice and love. The etymology explains why the goddess Frigg was the Old Norse equivalent of Venus, the goddess of love in Roman mythology. Perhaps Fridays (the name derived from Frigg) are for lovers—and marriage is an act of freedom that allows us to gain the roots that we need to keep from being blown around by ideological winds.

In the movie *Braveheart*, when William Wallace (played by Mel Gibson) under torture near the end yells "Freedom" and envisions his murdered wife, he is thinking as a Celt would have. Despite their typical depiction in most other contemporary American movies, families are places of freedom. Instead of being driven by loneliness to spend the evening with strangers, free people are devoted to each other and feel at ease in familial company. Husbands and wives can only fully enjoy the freedom of marital bonds when they exercise self-restraint in regard to others who could readily become objects of lust.

Civilization is passed on in part when children who want to be free learn that self-restraint is the key to true liberty. Because we fall far short of how we should act, parents often do not succeed in teaching that to children. Teenagers (and sometimes parents as well) readily spot the flaws in parental tutelage. But if parents abdicate, children may never learn what real freedom is, and they'll accept the new mythology that it means not having character but being one.

Let's turn for a moment now to liberty. We don't have to delve back a millennium—only to the eighteenth century when the term was often used in years leading up to the American Revolution. For Christians such as Connecticut minister Levi Hart, natural man was a captive of sin, and "the whole plan of Redemption is comprised in procuring, preaching, and bestowing liberty to the captives."* Liberty means the opportunity to do what we ought to do, not the liberty to do what we might desire at the moment. If we constantly indulge ourselves, we are slaves of our wants.

---

*For more on eighteenth-century thought, see my book *Fighting for Liberty and Virtue* (Crossway, 1995).

The expression "life, liberty, and the pursuit of property" (or "happiness," as the Declaration of Independence put it) involves not three goals thrown together but a plan whereby one leads to the next. When God gives us life, He also gives us liberty to choose an occupation to follow, or (if we are constrained as well as supported by the existence of a family business) a way to pursue it. If we choose wisely, we will engage in activity that most likely leads to both property and happiness. Political philosopher Michael Novak has pointed out that in the Anglo-American tradition the goal has been liberty under law, not liberty from law.

To come at it one other way: The 1904 version of "America the Beautiful" proclaims, "Confirm thy soul in self-control, thy liberty in law." Liberty, self-control, and the external control of law all work together to keep us from being enslaved by our temporary desires. Two centuries ago, the antonym to "liberty" that sprang to people's lips was not "slavery" but "license." A free person stood in the middle of a spectrum, not tugged by one mob to embrace libertinism or by another mob to hug dictatorship and political slavery.

TODAY'S HYSTERICAL MEANING

Are we free today? In one sense, beyond a doubt. My grandparents, immigrants to America, grew up with no means to have professional entertainment within their home. My parents grew up with radio. I grew up with three or four television stations. My students have grown up with cable and too many stations to count, along with remote controls that allow for instant changes. They have grown up with portable CD players for personal music wherever they go. They have never known a time without legal and frequent abortion. In short, they have lived their whole lives in a pro-choice environment, whether the choice concerns TV shows or a woman's pregnancy.

Many students I have had are the children of divorce or of single parenting, and so they don't have familial constancy in their lives. The upbringing of most has been postmodern, with no clear sense of right and wrong. Most want liberty and desperately want it NOW, without waiting one more second for it. The most tuned-in advertising slogan of recent decades, whether relating to hamburgers or to life and death, is "Have it your way." The choice can be wise or foolish, reasoned or arbitrary, but our goal is to sing in a parody of Sinatra, "I did it (bought it, fought it, worked it, quirked it) my way."

A generation ago Bob Dylan sang that the answer was "blowin' in the wind." Many Americans found at the end of that gust not liberty but license: Have it your way, a different way every day of the year. Our liberty now is the liberty of leaves. Christians can point out that a truly free person is not blown around by breezes. We should also note the dangers of licentious liberty. But this is where God has providentially placed us, and we need to learn how to live in these curious surroundings.

Why? Why not preach hellfire on the streets? Why not conspire to set up a theocratic government, if that were possible? Why not demand to have it the Christian way because if we are fervent enough won't God bless us? No. God does not bless breast-beating when He has commanded us to stand our ground and be patient. And every time God's people found themselves to be a minority outside the holy land, that's exactly what God commanded.

That was certainly the case in Babylon, a most ungodly country. As Jeremiah wrote, the exiled Israelites were to build houses, plant gardens, and remember that they were now part of Babylonia: "In its welfare you will find your welfare." God did not order attacks on idol-laden temples. He also did not tell the Israelites to lose their distinctives and melt into the surrounding community; assemblies of believers then and now must aspire to high standards. Daniel offered his advice to Babylonian rulers and did not walk off in a huff when some ignored it. Later, the book of Esther tells how Mordecai, realizing that the king of Persia's proclamation was irreversible, looked for a counterweight in Persian law and custom.

The New Testament exhibits the same pattern of standing firm on rights and proclaiming the gospel at every opportunity, but not calling for insurrection or giving up. Almost 2,000 years ago, when surrounded by paganism, the apostle Paul demanded not revolution but his rights as a Roman citizen. And so we must learn to live in the liberty theme park, even as we seek to teach other inhabitants that all of us find true liberty only in Christ. Merely complaining about the false understanding of freedom will do little good. Only as we show in both word and deed what a true understanding of liberty looks like, will we help to transform a culture.

THROWING DOWN OUR BUCKETS

We need to understand that saying, "Thou shalt do X because God says so," leads to blank stares or incredulous glances. Moral absolutes resonate poorly among people who desire absolute freedom and have never heard G.K. Chesterton's wise reminder: "The point of having an open mind, like having an open mouth, is to close it on something solid." We should understand that in the American liberty theme park, we cannot eliminate the negative; so our realistic option is to emphasize the positive.

Booker T. Washington used to tell the story of a storm-tossed trans-Atlantic ship that had run out of drinking water as it approached the mouth of the Amazon River. The captain signaled to a passing boat his desperate need for water, only to receive this message: "Throw down your bucket where you are." A sailor lowered a bucket into what was still the Atlantic Ocean and pulled it back up; the flow of the Amazon was so strong that several miles out to sea the water was fresh. And so we should throw down our buckets, seeing how we can expand homeschooling, give school vouchers a fighting chance, offer addicts faith-based anti-addiction programs along with conventional ones, and teach intelligent design alongside evolution.

The Brooklyn museum demonstrators, instead of playing into the choice versus repression formula, would have been more effective by emphasizing that $7 million given to a perverse clique means that less money is available for art education in schools or for more diverse exhibits elsewhere. They could have pointed out that government funding means less choice, not more, because it enables a small group of museum directors and their allies to decide what others will be able to see. The protesters had many options once they understood that anything that seems to remove choice is doomed to defeat.

Those who proclaim America the new Israel are also likely to lose. Around two decades ago, desperate to stem the tide of licentiousness, some Christians talked as if God had promised that the United States would be a Christian nation. Groups such as the Moral Majority promised that a full-court press would force secularists to turn over the ball. But there was no moral majority, sometimes not even within churches. Christian attempts to fight divorce on demand lost credibility as it became clear that many church members were divorcing as church leaders stood by.

Because the Bible teaches us that there is only one way to heaven, some Christians who become politically active equate politics (and their particular brand of it) as *the* only right way to bring about change. But God calls all of us to different tasks. Those who believe in the Bible are a minority, and Christians need to emphasize minority rights. Some Christians still say that we are letting God down if we don't buy their particular strategy of how to gain political dominance. Since God accomplishes His purposes regardless of where the votes lie, we should stop assuming—lest we doubt His power—that one of His purposes is to turn the United States into the United Christendom.

We are called to very high standards in our own lives and churches. We are called, through God's grace, to teach and disciple, explaining to a needy world a better way to live. We can be confident that God's way is the better way because God created the world and knows what works best for His creatures to live happily in it. For that reason, many politically correct activities are pragmatically incorrect.

Cruising homosexuals have a low life expectancy, even when AIDS is factored out. Abortion kills children and also psychologically and sometimes physically injures their mothers. Divorce leaves not only children but ex-partners in misery. We should note the consequences and try to lead secularists to living water, while remembering that we cannot make them drink.

Let's look for the silver (or at least rhinestone) linings in the dark clouds of postmodernism. We used to have to fight monolithic modernism, but now the monolith is pulled down, and choice is god. Since the major political rule in our liberty theme park is that he who talks of expanding choices normally wins, let's use that attitude to help Bible-based ideas gain a foothold. Let's be more postmodern than the postmodernists in many areas of public life. Are school administrators, under pressure, now saying that parents may choose among all public schools in a district? Fine, let them choose among all schools through the provision of vouchers or tax credits.

FIGHTING ABORTION IN THE LIBERTY THEME PARK

Abortion is a case in point of the difference that understanding Babylon can make. Let's start with the pro-life side, much of which is based in biblical belief and has a straightforward understanding. The Bible says you shall not murder. The Bible also clearly refers to preborn human life as human life. Ergo, we shall not murder those not yet born. Since we have laws against murder even in our liberty theme park, we should have laws against abortion.

The other side has two positions. One is that unborn human life is not really human life (but that has become less credible as wonderful photographs of unborn children have become widely available). The other is utilitarian: To go through with a pregnancy will ruin the life prospects of the mother.

To claim that unborn human life is not truly human life has become particularly hard to maintain among pregnant women who—hooked up to ultrasound machines that safely bounce sound waves off their unborn children—see sonograms of their children on a TV monitor. Dozens of crisis pregnancy centers have found that when a woman thinking about abortion sees a sonogram of her unborn child, the image frequently creates a bond that gives a troubled woman new courage to carry out the pregnancy. When the men involved see the sonogram, many also change their minds about abortion. As the Dallas Pregnancy Resource Center concluded, "Offering a pamphlet displaying fetal development promotes truth, but offering a sonogram displaying the beating heart of a woman's own child displays personal reality."

Today's ultrasound machines yield clearer pictures than those of a generation ago. Yet even those images helped Dr. Bernard Nathanson, after performing some 60,000 abortions, to perceive an unborn child's silent scream and join the pro-life side. The quality of sonograms has also improved enormously since the CBS morning news in 1998 featured a mother telling an interviewer how "when I had the ultrasound and actually saw the baby—that was when I bought into the idea that this was my child." As expensive as high-quality ultrasound machines are, they are the best way to make sure that adults cannot maintain a childlike naïveté about the effects of their actions. Since "personal reality" trumps all else in the liberty theme park, the pro-life movement would do well to make universal provision of sonograms a top priority.

It's vital as well to learn from history. Nineteenth-century pro-life leaders appreciated the usefulness of laws protecting unborn children but did not depend on them. Instead of complaining incessantly about the lack of enforcement of laws, they concentrated on ways to help women avoid abortion. These men and women emphasized abstinence, set up refuges for pregnant women, and helped them place babies for adoption. Their goals were pragmatic: Get abortionists off the streets and into either jail or a decent occupation. States frequently gave women immunity from all prosecution in exchange for testimony. Even prostitutes, who made up a majority of most abortionists' clients, were not jailed for abortions they had because legislatures wanted their help in nailing the abortionists. The goal of legislation was not to punish women but to contain the evil empire of the abortionists and to signal its illegitimacy.

Legislation was education, and nineteenth-century journalists also helped. In 1890, the *New York Times* described one abortionist, a Dr. McGonegal, as having "the appearance of a vulture. . . . His sharp eyes glitter from either side of his beaked nose, and cunning and greed are written all over his face." The *Times* in those days called abortion "the evil of the age" and sent reporters undercover into abortionist businesses to describe vividly the killing fields. Today's leading reporters (especially at the *Times*) have a different sensibility. Condemn the abortionist who provides choice? No way. But perhaps entrepreneurial journalists at other publications will find a way.

Those who value life have tried and failed for three decades to turn around or counter the Supreme Court's 1973 *Roe v. Wade* decision. With political and legal action stalled, an alternative approach begins with understanding the plight of the young women surprised by pregnancy. They now are likely to see abortion as the taking of human life, but to view it as sadly justifiable homicide, self-defense against tiny intruders who will ruin their lives—no more education, no career, no more boyfriends—unless the babies' lives are snuffed out. If these women don't abort, their crisis pregnancies will be followed by crisis infancies and crisis childhoods and crisis adolescence. They fear that they'll be doing it by themselves, with no husbands, no backup.

From their perspective, they can reluctantly choose legal homicide, or they can suffer the life imprisonment of single parenthood. Sadly, our society has minimized a third choice, adoption. That's the altruistic choice—a secure life for a child, often a gift to a childless couple—but teenagers generally ask not what they can do for others. We need to do more to encourage adoption in every way, but we haven't concentrated on that sufficiently because we have emphasized attempts to reduce the two choices, abortion or parenting, to one choice, a constitutional amendment prohibiting abortion.

Such an amendment is what all who are committed to life and true liberty hope for, but in our new Babylon, with choice as a god-word, the pro-life movement needs to be even more pro-choice than so-called pro-choicers. Christians need to campaign to double the choice, going from two—reluctant homicide or life imprisonment—to four, adding adoption and emphasizing marriage when appropriate and possible. With two main choices over the past quarter-century, about 50 percent of unmarried pregnancies have ended in abortion. With four choices, that figure could be reduced to 25 percent, saving hundreds of thousands of lives in the process. At that point it will be culturally and politically possible to remove the choice that eliminates the opportunity for preborn babies to one day grow up and make their own choices.

SIX MEDIA MISUNDERSTANDINGS

Christians are citizens of the United States and also citizens of God's kingdom. With that dual citizenship, some have the tendency to assume too much about what we can accomplish societally in our American Babylon. Some pile up strict rules as if conformity to outside pressure is the ladder to heaven. Most Christians, though, follow God's instructions by praying for America's welfare and by building families, homes, and businesses. Most understand that the Bible emphasizes a relationship with God, not a set of rules.

Coming to Christianity from the outside, I can still be as exasperated as some secular journalists by the actions of some Christians. While editing *World* during the past decade, though, I've seen that biblical Christians generally are well-prepared to use liberty theme park analysis. That's because six conventional press descriptions of Christians are simply not true for most.

1. *Anti-choice.* Going beyond abortion, we ourselves are used to choice. We like our dozens or hundreds of digital TV choices, music

choices, sports choices, food choices. We are pro-choice in not only shopping for goods but also shopping for schools. We want private schools to be an option for everyone, not just for the rich. We want theories of intelligent design to be taught alongside theories of evolution. We are pro-choice concerning social services; so we want addicts, alcoholics, and others to be offered faith-based programs along with conventional liberal ones. We don't want the poor or anyone to become dependent on government for biweekly bread because when we are dependent, we can no longer make free choices.

2. *Stuck on morality-legislating panaceas.* Christians are actually less likely than others to fixate on particular bills because we believe that triumph will come only when Christ returns. We know that sin cannot be wiped out because it is within everyone; we just don't want sin to gain governmental backing. We're not suckers for government-surplus stain removers that in practice grind the evil deeper into the social fabric. We believe that God instituted government for the prosecution of wrongdoers, not the promotion of evil. We are not trying to gain power to force change on millions from the top down because (among other reasons) we know that does not work. We do not believe that by societal restructuring we can liberate the natural "goodness" of man because we don't believe that natural goodness exists.

3. *Opposed to the First Amendment's guarantee of religious freedom.* No, we want the First Amendment to be a protection for the free expression of religious beliefs as it was intended to be. James Madison, its author, assured members of Congress that its purpose was to keep federal officials from placing on a pedestal one particular sect "to which they would compel others to conform." We believe that Congress should stay out of religious matters. We believe that Christians should not fear competition from other religions; we merely insist on a level playing field.

4. *Opposed to diversity.* No, we so truly believe in the importance of diversity that we do not want it to be only skin deep. God created

all kinds of people, all made in His image; so as we learn about and appreciate others, we also appreciate God. Churches have often failed in such reaching out, but things are improving. We also hope for improvements in media, academic, and governmental circles. We would like to see in the press fair treatment of a diversity of views, not just a stultifying extension of politically correct secular liberalism. We would like to reduce discrimination against Christians at colleges and universities. We would like to see welfare programs that honor religious diversity replace governmental one-size-fits-all approaches.

5. *Gullible followers of potential dictators.* No, we are less likely than others to bow down to any human authority. We obey a higher authority. We are taught not to put our trust in princes. We are political skeptics in relation to Washington orthodoxy. We are strict constructionists concerning both the Bible and the Constitution. We read the Bible to learn what God says, not what thoroughly modern millennialists wish He would say. We read the Constitution to see what the nation agreed to in 1787 and what the nation has changed in it through the amendment process. We know that more centralized power brings more reason for bribery and bribes (or large payments for "access"). We don't want judges to legislate for us.

6. *Pessimistic.* Actually, we're long-term optimists because we know that Christ will return someday, and many of us are short-term optimists as well. We believe in the dreams that our grandparents had. We love being in a country where we can freely worship and work, building families, churches, and businesses. In recent years we have seen the downfall of the Soviet empire, the containment of the welfare empire, and the advent of a faith-based initiative. Most of us believe, with all the disappointments, that the involvement of Christians and conservatives in politics over the past two decades has made a big difference in containing abortion, defending Christian and home schooling, and stiffening our backs in the face of terrorism.

PATIENCE IN AN IMPATIENT SOCIETY

Another quality found among those with a biblical focus is also vital for Christians living in Babylon— patience. Since secular liberals typically portray Christians as impatiently and unhappily hurling epithets at opponents, this word needs some definition. We are not called to procrastinate concerning sin in our own lives, families, and churches. We try to hold political leaders to their promises—and perhaps, through that tendency, teach candidates not to over-promise. Just as Christians in the Lord's Prayer ask God not to lead us into temptation, we try not to establish concentrations of political power that lead almost every office-holder into temptation. We recognize that history is full of examples of insurrectionists who, when they gained power, become imitators of what they overthrew. Russians in the 1970s joked about Leonid Brezhnev showing off his big homes and abundant possessions to his impressed mother, who then asked a worried question, "But what if the Communists come?"

A parallel question could be addressed to a few of the fire-breathing first-term congressmen from 1995 who have now adopted the ways of Washington and over-compromised: "But what if the Republican Revolution arrives?" Sure, it's disappointing that some leaders and followers breathed fire when fashionable and once in office made new alliances with the smoke detector industry. What impresses many Christians, though, is not that the go-along get-alongs exist, but that many principled conservatives have stood fast.

It has been that way throughout American history. What surprises me, looking back, is that nineteenth-century leaders like Andrew Jackson and Grover Cleveland stood up against centralizing pressures. When they ran for reelection, they had to fight the tendency of some of their followers to be frustrated because their main White House successes lay not so much in pushing a new agenda as in stopping bad things from happening.

It's not surprising that conservatives haven't won the ballgame. It's surprising that after a century of political centralization, we still have a ballgame. After all, throughout the century we've seen decades of liberalism (the 1910s, 1930s, and 1960s in particular) followed by periods not of roll-back conservatism but of consolidation. Presidents such as Calvin Coolidge in the 1920s and Ronald Reagan in the 1980s were willing to stand athwart history and say no. Both times, however, weak successors were unable to stay the course, and the next decade witnessed new expansions of governmental power.

It's not surprising that changing a political culture is very hard and that a century-long movement takes more than a few years to reverse. Of course some congressmen who come to Washington committed to decentralization fall into the old pattern of thinking that if they favor a particular human need or desire, they should vote to spend tax money on it. Bible-centered Christians, however, do not see that as reason to give up.

I've personally seen progress in the war of ideas. In 1989 talk in Washington about the crucial role of churches in fighting poverty and crime was seen as a brave but way-out prophecy. But a decade later *Newsweek* had a cover headline that proclaimed, "God vs. Gangs. What's the Hottest Idea in Crime Fighting? The Power of Religion." In 1992 the prospects for attaining serious welfare reform seemed almost nil. Now the welfare changes of 1996 have led to the fewest number of welfare cases since the 1960s. Politicians of many stripes emphasize effective compassion, at least rhetorically, rather than mere material distribution.

In 1995, when my then-ten-year-old son Daniel told a group of liberal political dignitaries that he was being educated in homeschool, many had never heard of that notion; several asked, "Charm school?" Now even establishment publications such as *Education Week* and *Newsweek* are giving homeschoolers respectful attention.

A change in dominant ideas eventually leads to political change, but the transition takes time. Most Christians, in my experience, are willing to be patient. A few Christians, discouraged, slap on bumper stickers like this one: "Don't vote; it will just encourage them." But most suggest to our fellow theme park residents, "Vote for the good ones. It'll encourage them."

The number of religious readers who think our society is sinking fast has been sufficient to make books such as the *Left Behind* series huge bestsellers. Yet even those popular futuristic novels have an optimistic aspect. The good guys fight back and often succeed. Christians who don't expect imminent upheaval are even more optimistic that many Americans will either maintain or gain belief in Christ. True, the religious currents that ran fast after 9/11 slowed down once many were no longer pushed to prayer by the feeling of being preyed upon. Still, it's likely that in the uncertain world of the next decade most Americans will once again find themselves clinging to a rock, either the true one—Christ—or an imagined one.

Christians also realize that whether or not terrorists mind their manners, one grim reaping will advance: Baby boomers are aging. By the sheer demographic numbers they have yanked press chains for a third of a century, from college protests in the 1960s and diet books in the 1980s to Viagra in the 1990s—all becoming big news. Interest in religion generally increases as people age. We may also note greater interest in the impact of religion on life as we see how different religions lead some of our new neighbors to act in dramatically different ways. The number of Hindus, Buddhists, and Muslims in America has increased sixfold during the past thirty years, which means that religions once exotic in America are now next door to us. All this increases public interest about how faiths affect people's lives.

Overall, these factors lead to movement away from what Richard John Neuhaus called "the naked public square," naked in its lack of religious discussion. We've learned over the past four decades that attempts to avoid mentioning religion in public places do not yield neutrality; they leave us naked. We have lived in a society, unusual in the history of the world, where many intellectual leaders boasted of nakedness. Most people in most places at most times have worn religious clothes, and as many Americans face pressure—perhaps from terrorists but certainly from the terror of growing old—that is likely to be the case again.

None of these trends guarantee a greater number of adherents to Christianity, but they suggest opportunities for those who are bold and honest. Christians know that sin cannot be eradicated in this life, only contained. A religion that says the best people do not sin leads to pride and closed mouths. Christianity's understanding that all of us sin and that all sins are covered by Christ's sacrifice leads to self-criticism and the willingness to change. Christians know that people can change anytime, for God changes millions from the inside out, transforming hearts and minds in a way that leads to a rethinking of how to live.

MAINTAINING LIBERTY AND FIGHTING DETERMINISM

Fatalism, the idea that some people are destined for trouble and that it's useless to take action to fight the descent, opposes the Christian concept that attitudes and lives can change. A staple of Greek and Roman belief, fatalism still figures prominently in Hinduism ("karma"), Islam ("kismet"), and many tribal religions, but it's also evident in many media presentations today. We are stuck in a rut.

The difference between fatalism and the Christian concept of providence is illustrated by a story about one of Stonewall Jackson's aides, Presbyterian minister Robert L. Dabney. One day in 1862 Dabney preached a sermon on God's "special providence," noting that in a recent battle "Every shot and shell and bullet was directed by the God of battles." Not much later Dabney found himself under fire and took cover behind a large gatepost. A nearby officer kidded him: "If the God of battles directs every shot, why do you want to put a gate-post between you and a special providence?" Dabney replied, "Just here the gate-post is the special providence."

Fatalism versus providence: The contrast is clear even in sports where victories depend on players stepping up rather than fatalistically going through the motions. Johnny Oates, a former Texas

Rangers manager who lost his life through cancer but did not lose his faith, put this well in a spring-training conversation we had a decade ago. He said, "We play aggressively; I never want any Christian to be passive and start saying, 'It's God's will.' Our goal is to do everything in our power that's not morally wrong or illegal to win a ballgame. Second, if we lose, I tell the players, 'Go look at yourself in the mirror. If you did everything you could, go home and get a good night's rest. If not, remember what you did wrong; then go home and rest.'"

That proper understanding of providence allows for individual initiative, because never-give-up individual action feeds into the ordained outcome. It suggests prudent risk-taking, not a clinging to what is current for fear of any change. It leads brave people to take action when children are about to die either physically or psychologically. Only when we've done all we can and failed do we know that a death was ordained.

Ted Yamamori, former head of the Christian relief agency Food for the Hungry, once described an African woman who was mourning the death of her child. The youngster was sick but still alive; yet the mother was convinced that fate decreed her child's death. Yamamori changed fate by getting the child medicine that restored him to health. We in the liberty theme park have similar opportunities to save children shuttled from foster home to foster home until they lose any sense of continuity and trust. Almost miraculously, a home with patient, compassionate parents can often bring them back from the brink of emotional death. A fatalist might say that such troubled children are fated to a life of misery, but two parents can become their protecting gateposts and change these children's lives.

A good example of how this principle works out in practice now comes from the little town of Clio, Michigan, just north of the city of Flint. Clio is home for thirty-year-old Jerod Montague, born with cerebral palsy, and his parents. Jerod is cheerful but cannot walk, talk, or go to the bathroom by himself. His parents, in their fifties, have cared for Jerod for three decades; Jim Montague uses his liberty to head a company that manufactures precision parts for everything from locks and latches to washing machines. He has also used profits from the Montague Tool & Manufacturing Company to develop a way to help not only his son but the children of others. Mr. and Mrs. Montague are building a $2 million home next to their own home that will have room for Jerod, along with eight others who have cerebral palsy, plus living quarters for house parents and nursing help.

The Montagues have devoted themselves to each other and to their son, and now they are using their freedom to expand their circle of benevolence. Their goal is to make parents feel at ease, in accordance with the mission statement they provide: "We believe God doesn't make mistakes. . . . It is a high calling to provide quality care to those physically and mentally challenged in such a way that would be pleasing and honoring to our Heavenly Father and bring emotional and spiritual healing to those who brought them into this world." No one told the Montagues to build a home for those with cerebral palsy. They did it on their own, using profits they had been able to retain from their business. They wanted to do it because they read the Bible and decided to put into practice its teaching about loving our neighbors' sons as our own sons. With freedom, they built ties that bind people in love.

Today, some sophisticated ideologues contend that individuals cannot change lives, but masses of individuals can. Marxism emphasizes class identity: Bourgeoisie (the middle class) and proletarians (the working class) can never see eye to eye because their eyes see fundamentally different things. Providentially, that notion of class consciousness ("It's a proletarian thing you wouldn't understand") has been discredited all over the world, not only by the failure of socialistic practice but by observation of individual beliefs. Attitudes vary widely among workers, as they do among people of any particular race. Marxists try to account for such variance by saying that some workers identify with their bourgeois oppressors ("false consciousness"), but that game grew old.

The new game in university towns is neo-Marxism, which emphasizes, instead of class identity, markers such as race, sex, and sexual preference. The theory is twisted predestinarian: People think as they do because they are x, y, or z, since a specific consciousness goes with belonging to a particular group. The rhetorical advantages of neo-Marxism are numerous. Adherents can maintain traditional left-wing values by thundering as their Marxist fathers did about oppressed groups of people. Marxist diatribes can be recycled. Just substitute "people of color" for the working class, "angry white males" for the bourgeoisie, and "homophobes" for any other old-time villains.

Ludicrous? Yes, as Karl Marx wrote in one essay comparing the mid-nineteenth-century Napoleon III with the original Napoleon, what emerged the first time as tragedy may come back later as farce. But farces can be serious. For example, "critical race theory," the view that there are competing and irreconcilable racial views of reality, played a key role in O. J. Simpson's criminal trial. Lawyers successfully swayed a jury to ignore evidence and acquit a man who suddenly became not a murderer in their eyes but the victim of a racist police force. The jury in that case ignored important facts, but University of Virginia Professor Alex M. Johnson Jr. claimed that the "voice of color . . . rejects narrow evidentiary concepts of relevance and credibility."

Neo-Marxists contend that blood is thicker than truth, and people don't have the liberty to change. Such determinism works well within the emphasis on group identity that is central to multiculturalism: Its devotees want the liberty theme park to give special rates for group tours. Because neo-Marxism is inconsistent with the theme park's emphasis on individual liberty, Christians who take the lead in opposing this ideology often find support from other Americans. The Crips and the Bloods are infamous in the annals of gang warfare, and the twenty-first century may see a gang-like battle of scholarly Bloods (who emphasize thought linked to race, ethnicity, and gender) versus Scrips (who read Scripture and recognize that ideas, not collectivities, are paramount). Christians who show courage can win this contest because neo-Marxists, like their Marxist predecessors, are fighting the current of liberty that runs strongly in all our theme park rivers.

CONTENTMENT AMID DISTRESS

If Christians talk back to the Babylonians while following Jeremiah's instructions to build homes and tend gardens, will that prevent trouble? Not if we are faithful to God. Daniel and his friends minded their own business as they followed their callings as governmental advisors, but Daniel was thrown into a lion's den and his friends into a blazing furnace. Living in the liberty theme park does not mean becoming dainty and docile, rewriting the Bible so that Moses follows the crowd and worships the golden calf, David plays his harp for Goliath, and Elijah becomes associate pastor at the church of Baal.

The dramatic nature of Christ's claims means that life as a Christian in Babylon is not boring. Christ's statement, "I am the way," means that other ways are not, and that does not sit well with some. Christianity cannot be the live-and-let-live religion that goes down easily in a theologically laid-back society because Christians know that the reality apart from God is live-and-let-die. Christ's claims inevitably force a reaction, either believing or hostile, just as He said they would.

Christians, of course, face pressures to appease the Babylonians. A forthright Christian student taking a test or writing a term paper for an adversarial professor has to count the cost. He may be graded down for taking a stand for Christ. A Christian humanities or social sciences professor writing an article has to count the cost. If he is "a fool for Christ," his colleagues might consider him simply a fool. A Christian talking to her non-Christian parent has to count the cost. If she talks about Jesus, her mom will think her weird. In a secular liberal culture, we often get along better with neighbors and relatives, in the short term, if we do not in any way seem threatening.

Living in the liberty theme park does not mean being personally obnoxious. Whether we are presenting the gospel or a Bible-based political position, we should search out points of contact, fighting hard but fighting smart. We should learn about our Babylonian culture, as Daniel did about his. But whether or not we are stand-up Christians or stand-up comics depends on whose applause we covet and how desperately we desire to become members of certain clubs.

Garrison Keillor several years back contrasted Minneapolis, which he said wanted to be hip, with its twin city St. Paul, apparently content to be square. Mr. Keillor wrote that "Minneapolis, not St. Paul, is a mecca for performance artists, people who can't sing or dance or write or act but who can crawl through a pile of truck tires wearing a shower curtain. . . . Minneapolitans lean forward and watch them, perspiring, afraid that some subtlety may escape them. St. Paulites look at each other and say, 'Whose idea was this?'"

The original St. Paul gave a hip performance for a while in Acts 17, impressing the elite of Athens. But then—inexplicably by worldly standards—he blew it by talking about the resurrection of the dead. Several Athenians did come to believe, but Paul gave up his opportunity to win broad Areopagus acclaim. Every Christian intellectual, every Christian journalist, every Christian in the liberty theme park faces that same temptation: to become (within the Keillor framework) a Minneapolitan.

If we stand, will we be content, when we could be going on a variety of rides in our liberty theme park? After all, theme parks are not always the happiest places on earth. Adults and children may bake on hot pavement after paying steep prices for thrills that last a few minutes and standing in lines that last far longer. Meanwhile, VIPs go to the head of the line or are even rich enough to build their own roller coasters. Some rides end in disaster and mangled bodies. Sometimes we ourselves, or our children, crash.

Joachim Neander's children were the victims of a fatal crash over three centuries ago. He wrote a hymn still sung today, "Praise to the

Lord," that includes the line, "How oft in grief hath not He brought thee relief, spreading His wings to o'er shade thee." Christian, the hero of *The Pilgrim's Progress*, regularly had grief followed by relief, and that often seems to be what God ordains. As Christians we learn that if we expect life to go smoothly, we will spend much of it discontented, and we won't come to understand God's mercy.

It's hard to accept that the road to contentment runs through misery. Christ came to earth not only to die but also to live amid rejection. His horribly painful death on Good Friday took several hours. It was terrible physically, spiritually, and psychologically, but think also of the rejection that occurred during the night before the crucifixion and all the rejections that occurred prior to Good Friday—rejections by family, by community, by local religious leaders, by national religious leaders. Those also were painful. Much of the Bible is about the painful rejection of prophets and even of God's grace.

So, for that matter, is much of human history. *Foxe's Book of Martyrs*, the great sixteenth-century journalistic/historical account, reports the persecution of Christians through the ages. Paul Johnson's book *Modern Times*, a history of the twentieth century, implicitly shows the rejection of God during that time. Friedrich Nietzsche a century ago, and Ted Turner more recently, snarled that Christianity is a religion for losers. Christians who understand that the last will be first know that those two snarlers were wrong, but Christianity is certainly a religion that understands the reality of rejection.

Christianity is also a religion of contentment amid distress. Here's one of the last pieces of advice in a great book penned by Jeremiah Burroughs during the 1640s, *The Rare Jewel of Christian Contentment*: "Make a good interpretation of God's ways toward you." Burroughs taught that those who have some trouble or fail a test should think that God perhaps has provided a trial to build character. Perhaps hearts were inordinately set on a selfish goal. Perhaps success would have created opportunities to fall into sin. Perhaps God was preparing the afflicted for some great work or setting the stage for some great grace. Burroughs offers each whiner a challenge: If you put all the miseries of the world in one huge heap and divided them up equally among everyone on the globe, would you have fewer?

Advertising messages within our liberty theme park suggest thousands of times a day that any misery we feel is due to our external environment and that buying a change in that environment will give us contentment. But Christianity emphasizes the internal state. If we think we are discontent because we don't have enough goods, we should realize that taking in air does not satisfy the stomach, and taking in things does not satisfy the soul. Burroughs provides the solution to discontent: "not in bringing anything from outside to make my condition more comfortable, but in purging out something that is within." Today we might say instead of buying a more prestigious car, purge covetousness by taking delight in what God already has bestowed on us. Instead of checking out Internet pornography, purge lust by enjoying rightful pleasures.

That is a message today's Babylonians need to hear and to see Christians practice. Here's what the apostle Paul wrote at the beginning of chapter 12 in his letter to the Romans: ". . . I urge you, brothers, in view of God's mercy, to offer your bodies as living sacrifices, holy and pleasing to God—this is your spiritual act of worship. Do not conform any longer to the pattern of this world, but be transformed by the renewing of your mind. Then you will be able to test and approve what God's will is—his good, pleasing and perfect will" (vv. 1-3 NIV).

2

MEETING THE PRESS

Ten years ago I ran across a program for adults with IQs far below normal that trained them to be baggers at supermarkets. What made the program work was its retraining component. Graduates of the program did a decent job, but every few months they would start putting the milk on top of the bread and would then need a refresher course. Realizing their need, the baggers were ready to learn. All of us should be so willing to listen, even to journalists (maybe especially to journalists) who tell us that we're putting the milk on top of the bread.

Jeremiah Burroughs wrote, "If you hear others report this or that ill of you, and your hearts are dejected because you think you suffer in your name, your hearts were inordinately set on your name and reputation." Sometimes we need to have lower self-esteem. In the Old Testament, David reacted properly to Shimei who cursed him, threw stones at him, and flung dust at him—because David discerned that Shimei actually was God's instrument. Instead of living by whine and cheesy complaints, we should listen to criticism and not overstate our plight.

So, what can we learn from our journalistic Shimeis? First, it's clear that fringe fundamentalists have given liberal journalists plenty of ammunition. Like the rest of us, journalists have seen video clips of a small group that appears at gay gathering places to yell, "God hates fags"—and as columnist Walter Lippmann wrote in the 1920s, the "pictures in our head" are more vivid than the action before our eyes. Journalists who picture Christians as haters ignore the work of evangelicals who help homosexuals stricken with AIDS. (Those groups, of course, are anathema to gay militants since these believers still regard homosexual activity as sin.)

We cannot blame everything, however, on a few screamers at the edge. Major fundamentalist churches have at times added to biblical rules man-made ones against dancing, card-playing, listening to particular types of music, drinking a beer, and so on. These extra-biblical restrictions have a long heritage—even Oliver Cromwell imposed some in England during the 1650s—but they produce confusion about what is truly of God and what is merely of man. Often these types of rules emerge from good motives and are developed for the same reasons Orthodox Jews develop their restrictions: to set up the fence so far from the border that there is no possibility of anyone stepping over. Yet rules often produce an adversarial reaction, as Cromwell found out.

Restrictions about dancing and music are now unusual, but many Washington journalists I spoke with in 1999 and 2000 thought that just about every church has them. Those tendencies and others lead to press stereotypes of Christians, some of which are largely accurate. Mockery (including self-mockery) is the leading form of humor for David Letterman and others on television after early-to-rise folks have gone to bed, and Christians do tend to be straitlaced by contemporary standards. That's all to the good, as long as the laces keep our shoes on and don't trip us up. But often they do trip us, and then we need to go by the Bible, not some customs developed in the nineteenth century.

We need to acknowledge that until recent years many white members of Christian churches harassed blacks, and racial prejudice still exists. We should listen to the accusations of Shimeis that members of affluent churches have turned their backs on the poor. None of this is surprising—Christians know that "all have sinned and fall short of the glory of God"—but we need to repent. (Repentance means more than feeling sorry because we're caught, but realizing that we have offended God and must pray for the grace to turn about and change our ways.)

We should also keep in mind a stylistic difference between many evangelicals and the many journalists trained on David Letterman mockery. A typical Washington journalist looks down on Christians who have such a sincere desire to reach the non-Christian that they start talking *at* him rather than reasoning *with* him. Proselytizing styles often grate. Christians need to remember that God's action changes lives, not our strategy or intensity. Many journalists tell privately of their experience with evangelicals who refused to take no for an answer and pushed even harder when rejection was apparent. (That impoliteness may stem from a lack of confidence in Christ, because this year's no is never a final answer to those He calls.)

HOW TO BE A STRICT CONSTRUCTIONIST: THE RAPIDS TEST

Christianity is inevitably offensive to secular journalists, but we only honor God when we are offensive for the right reasons. If we are personally obnoxious, or if we say, "God says," when He hasn't, then we are disgracing rather than embracing Christ. At the same time, it's vital not to back off from politely telling the truth about God and the principles He has established, which are of benefit to all. We should not be defensive in proclaiming that the Bible is for everyone. God created the world, and He's the only one who knows how it objectively works. The most reasonable thing man can do is to follow what He says.

Few journalists understand that. Reporters have asked me countless times for a particular verse in the Bible that made me come to a specific cultural or political position, as if Christians are always looking merely to quote a Scripture verse and go home. I try to explain that while Scripture memorization is very useful, it's often more important in making applications to have read big chunks of the Bible over and over throughout the years. That helps us to be strict constructionists of Scripture, neither overusing Scripture by stating that a clear biblical position exists when one does not, nor under-using it by pretending that defining right and wrong in a specific instance is up to us when God has provided clear teaching.

Overuse and under-use are the Scylla and Charybdis of biblical application. We can navigate our way through with the help of a watery metaphor based on whitewater rafting. Experts talk of six classes of rapids, from class one (easy enough for a novice) to class six (death with a roar).

A class one rapids issue is one on which the Bible is explicit: Murder, adultery, theft, and other sins clearly and specifically identified in the Bible are wrong. Christians should be forthright in identifying these as sins. Tone is important; ranting by the gate of the liberty theme park tends to be far less effective than pointing out the sad consequences of adultery and then explaining why we see such consequences. We should explain that God understands intimately our human nature and so gave us laws that fit it. Class two issues involve an implicit biblical position—for example, that Christian children should receive a Bible-based education or that preborn children deserve protection from the moment God weaves them intricately in their mothers' wombs (Psalm 139).

Clarity decreases progressively with other rapids classes. Regarding class three issues, partisans of both sides can quote Bible verses, but careful study allows biblical conclusions. Welfare reform is an example: Partisans of government entitlements cite biblical verses about the need for compassion toward the poor, but it's also important to bring out biblical teaching about how compassion should be applied. The Bible emphasizes challenging, personal, and spiritual help, and those who merely enable the poor to stay in poverty are going against God. In explaining this fact, we need to present biblical teaching along with examples of how liberal ideological constructs concerning crime, homelessness, mental illness, education, and welfare produced awful consequences for the poor. (They did for the rich also, but a wealthy single mom has far more options than her impoverished counterpart.)

Class four issues do not provide us with clear biblical mandates but do allow us to bring to bear a biblical understanding of human nature. For example, the human body is beautiful, and there's nothing wrong in principle with painting and sculpting nudes, but an awareness of our prurient natures should push us to develop safeguards against our tendencies to turn good into evil. Food and drink are good, but left to our own devices, we tilt toward gluttony and drunkenness; so we should take precautions.

On class five issues we have no clear biblical mandates nor clear applications of the effect of human nature on an activity, but we do have historical experience concerning what works and what does not. For example, we have reason to be suspicious of the person who says, "I'm from the government, and I'm here to help you." We now have ample evidence that minimum wage laws, rent control, and other once-hailed policies do not help the poor. Over a century ago, Lord John Acton summarized his Bible-based understanding in these famous words: "Power corrupts, and [in man's hands] absolute power tends to corrupt absolutely."

Class six issues are those in which there is no clear biblical position or other clear indications; so people equally well-versed in the Bible will often take diametrically opposed positions. Technical economic issues—whether to raise or lower interest rates, for example— are often of this nature, as are complex questions of international diplomacy. Biblical understandings will often help analysts in sorting out the relevant questions, but Christians should be careful not to state that there is one biblical position on this subject to which all should ascribe or else.

We should fight the tendency among liberal Christians to think that every rapids is a class five or six. Discerning Christians who have immersed themselves in the Bible can paddle aggressively through most rapids without ending up in freezing water. Christ did not die for us so that we would be captives of fear. At the same time, it's important to remember that God has not spoken on every subject. Class one and two issues should be clear to all, but the others require considerable discernment and humility in staking out a claim. If we say, for example, that anyone who opposes our particular position on the Middle East is going against God, we are leading secular journalists and others to mock God.

HARASSMENT FROM THE *NEW YORK TIMES*

Having acknowledged errors among Christians, should we conclude that the most influential U.S. press organs are guiltless? Alas, no—not when Christians are lumped in with repressive forces from other cultures that have little in common with evangelicals. After the 9/11 disaster, journalists labeled Osama bin Laden an Islamic fundamentalist and argued or implied that other fundamentalists were also threats. Let's look at some examples of this broad religious profiling, starting with six (from among many) examples of bias displayed by the highly influential *New York Times* during the six months following the September attacks.

• Five days after 9/11, correspondent Serge Schmemann wrote that the terrorists opposed "values cherished in the West as freedom, tolerance, prosperity, religious pluralism and universal suffrage, but abhorred by religious fundamentalists (and not only Muslim fundamentalists) as licentiousness, corruption, greed and apostasy." His implication was clear: Conservative Christians in America associate liberty with licentiousness and prosperity with greed.

• The October 7, 2001, *New York Times* magazine ran an essay by Andrew Sullivan that labeled the war on terrorism "a religious war—but not of Islam versus Christianity and Judaism. Rather, it is a war of fundamentalism against faiths of all kinds that are at peace with freedom and modernity." His definition of fundamentalism: "The blind recourse to texts embraced as literal truth, the injunction to follow the commandments of God before anything else, the subjugation of reason and judgment and even conscience to the dictates of dogma." Among the blind subjugators of reason were fundamentalist Christians.

• *Times* columnist Thomas L. Friedman on November 27 wrote that Islam, Judaism, and Christianity all have to choose between "an ideology that accepts religious diversity" and the belief of "Christian and Jewish fundamentalists" that there is "just one religious path." The *Times* did print a letter by David Zwiebel of the Orthodox Jewish group Agudath Israel that took issue with Friedman's either-or stipulation. Zwiebel wrote that the "vision of America as a country where religious belief is welcome only if it abandons claims to exclusive truth is truly chilling—and truly intolerant."

• Fifty-year *Times* veteran Anthony Lewis, in his farewell column on December 15, 2001, wrote that "the phenomenon of religious fundamentalism is not to be found in Islam alone. Fundamentalist Christians in America, believing that the Bible's story of creation is the literal truth, question not only Darwin but the scientific method that has made contemporary civilization possible." In an interview the following day, Lewis equated Osama bin Laden and John Ashcroft as men sure of what they believe and thus supportive of indecent and inhumane policies, for "certainty is the enemy of decency and humanity in people who are sure they are right."

• *Times* columnist Bill Keller staked out a strong, early claim for the most mean-spirited column of 2002 when on January 12 he wrote of retiring senators Phil Gramm, Jesse Helms, and Strom Thurmond as having "harnessed their collective century of seniority to the Taliban wing of the American right." Keller complained specifically about items such as "our stingy foreign aid" but gave no evidence of any of the three having acted in any Taliban-type ways.

• *Times* columnist Maureen Dowd on March 21, 2002, equated biblical requirements concerning male leadership with "the Taliban obliteration of women." Stories about both U.S. and Islamic religious groups, she concluded, show "how twisted societies become when women are either never seen, dismissed as second-class citizens, or occluded by testosterone."

The *Times* led the way in trying to make millions of Americans believe that Bible-believing Christians are major threats to domestic tranquility. Christians should not whine about this, but should start by acknowledging what is accurate in the reports and noting the distortions. The Bible does teach certainty—Christ is *the* way, *the* truth, and *the* life. The Bible does teach that God created man male and female, that wives are to submit to their husbands as the church is to submit to Christ, that men are to be willing to die for their wives as Christ died for the church. A woman whose husband would die for her is no more a second-class citizen than the president of the United States who has Secret Service agents ready to die for him.

We should show with specific detail not only how the *Times* violates its own standards of fairness, but also how *Times* writers are inconsistent. "Certainty is the enemy of decency"? Lewis idolized Nelson Mandela in 1990, calling him "a man of extraordinary conviction and strength." Does Lewis now believe that only wimps should be trusted? A careful study of history would have shown him that decency and humanity hold out against barbarism only when their defenders are certain that these principles are worth defending. Osama bin Laden, after all, argued that the U.S. could readily be defeated because Americans hold no moral convictions.

Christians should suggest to Lewis that the real enemy of decency and humanity is ridicule of faith in God who made man in His own image. If we are merely chance collections of atoms, what decency and humanity do we inherently possess? Lewis's charge that critics of Darwin are anti-science should also be disproved by showing that conservative Christians have been the foremost defenders of the scientific method with its emphasis on laboratory experiments and careful observation. Proponents of "intelligent design" have been unwilling to accept on faith Darwin's conclusions since they cannot be tested in a lab.

HARASSMENT FROM OTHER PUBLICATIONS

Standing firm is also a good response to attacks in other publications that mirror the disdain of the *Times*, leader of the journalistic pack. Here are seven examples in other publications of the Taliban-Christian equation.

• A *Washington Post* article on December 30, 2001, postulated Christian-Muslim equivalence: "Today, there are Christian fundamentalists who attack abortion clinics in the United States and kill doctors; Muslim fundamentalists who wage their sectarian wars against each other . . ." Editors evidently saw no need to point out that the rare abortionist killings have been condemned widely within Christendom while the rampant rage within Islam has received broad encouragement.

• The *Washington Post* on January 17, 2002, noted that American "religious conservatives" opposed cloning while "At the same time, the United States was fighting a war to free a faraway nation from the grip of religious conservatives who were denounced for imposing their moral code on others." The *Post* reporter complained that support for protecting embryos "could legitimize an effort to codify fundamentalist views into law."

• The *Atlantic Monthly's* February 2002 cover story, "Oh, Gods!" ended with analysis of how fast Christianity is growing in Africa and South America, and suggested that concern about Islam is overblown, for "the big 'problem cult' of the twenty-first century will be Christianity."

• *Time* magazine writer Margaret Carlson complained on February 20 that John Ashcroft "has a history of using his bully pulpit, as Attorney General, as a pulpit. He has prayer sessions every morning in his office. He doesn't agree, apparently, with pluralism. . . . He believes that there is one form of religion . . . and it should be practiced as an official matter of state." Ashcroft, of course, has often said exactly the opposite, but Ms. Carlson apparently contends that a government official who prays in his office wants to be a religious dictator.

• The *Seattle Post-Intelligencer* on March 29 called Supreme Court Justices Rehnquist, Scalia, and Thomas "spiritual heroes to the Taliban wing of the Republican Party."

• Sometimes it's hard to know whether liberal publications start a trend and liberal politicians follow, or vice versa. *Newsweek*'s Howard Fineman reported on December 31, 2001, that Democrats would attack Republican candidates with charges that the GOP is "dependent upon an intolerant 'religious right.'" Democratic talking points when "comparing the GOP right with the Taliban," according to Mr. Fineman, will be: "Our enemy in Afghanistan is religious extremism and intolerance. It's therefore more important than ever to honor the ideals of tolerance—religious, sexual, racial, reproductive—at home." Was *Newsweek* reporting or suggesting?

• By August 2002, the equation was being used widely by journalists around the world who wanted to attack American foreign policy. Even Saudi Arabia's *al-Watan* newspaper was arguing, "Christian fundamentalism is no less dangerous to international peace and security than extremists in other religions. Rather it is more dangerous, especially if it controls the policy of the United States."

Look at the words journalists repeatedly use—*freedom, diversity, tolerance*. Those are god-words within the liberty theme park. Christians are said to oppose these concepts, but for the most part that's just not true. Sure, biblical Christians criticize both heterosexual adultery and homosexual practice. But Christians do not favor a sexual police force that would bust into bedrooms. Most are willing to tolerate the presence of adulterers and homosexuals. Most are unwilling, though, to affirm those practices as virtuous when the Bible clearly states they are sinful.

REFUSING TO MOVE

Based on these statements (which could be multiplied by the thousands), American Christians clearly face harassment. *Harass* means to impede by repeated raids, to exhaust, to fatigue. If we merely state what God says repeatedly in the Bible about sin and the need for grace, some journalists attack Christians as purveyors of "hate speech." Rebutting such charges get old, but we do have the opportunity to rebut within the liberty theme park, and rebut we must. The historical record shows that Christians who stand on constitutional rights of freedom to worship, speak, and write can fight back successfully. Silence equals defeat.

Sometimes boldness means staking out new territory, but sometimes it just means refusing to move. One of my favorite movie lines was uttered by Jefferson Smith (Jimmy Stewart) in *Mr. Smith Goes to Washington.* As senators were pleading with him to give up the floor when he began a filibuster, and some were trying to trick him with parliamentary maneuvers, he requested clarification of his position. Then, with the words, "As I was saying," he showed his resolve to continue the filibuster.

As I was saying—sometimes the best tactic is a simple refusal to change positions or seats. Think of Rosa Parks in 1955, who was a member of a harassed minority. She sat near the front of a bus in Montgomery, Alabama. When the bus driver told her to conform to segregation rules by moving to the back, she uttered two words: "I'm tired." Those words were the perfect expression of a harassed person. Rosa Parks was so exhausted that she was steadfast. By her refusal to move, she put into gear the modern civil rights movement.

Christians should refuse to move. We have the Bible, and we should not move from it. We need to point out press assaults without being surprised or unduly upset by them. After all, biblical Christians are used to being beaten up verbally. I had to get used to it. Early in 2000, because I was known as an advisor to George W. Bush and had publicly stated that men and women have some psychological as well as physical differences, feminists and their allies in *Newsweek* and other publications were harassing me. When the *Daily Texan*, the University of Texas student paper controlled that year by campus radicals, jumped on me also, I was feeling a bit blue. Then two things happened.

First, my youngest son, then nine, came to my office and saw that someone had painted in big block letters the word *PIG*. But the G looked like a 6, and my son asked, "Why did someone write P-16 on your door?" That put in perspective harassment by paint or threatening letters. Christians in other lands face sticks and stones; we face words.

Second, my wife and I went to have lunch on campus. Susan had the sensation that people were looking at us, maybe because the campus hit piece had just come out. While I was feeling a little rejected, she recalled how when she was a little girl, she loved going places with her grandpa. He was as tall as a maple tree, she thought. He was also very old—in his upper eighties at that time. She said that as they walked down the street, everyone would look at them, and she was so proud to be next to him just as she was proud to be next to me.

That was very sweet, but there's something far sweeter. The church is the bride of Christ, and when we are scorned and rejected because of that relationship, we should remember that we're walking down the street next to Christ, who is even taller than a maple tree. And we should refuse to move away from Christ.

STARING DOWN THE RANTS

When we keep in mind the great gift of grace, so what if Barbara Ehrenreich of *The Progressive* calls John Ashcroft a "Christian Wahhabist" (referring to Osama bin Laden's Islamic sect) and bin Laden an "Islamic Calvinist"? Ms. Ehrenreich long ago made up her mind that "Islamic and Christian fundamentalists" are all "crabbed and punitive in outlook." We should not be dismayed by the way newspapers become megaphones for abortionists like Warren Hearn;

dismayed when Colorado's governor cut state payments to Planned Parenthood, he said, "Governor Owens has brought the spirit of the Taliban to Colorado." We should stare down rants by the abortionist who told the St. Louis *Post-Dispatch* that antiabortionists "are no different than Osama bin Laden," or by the Planned Parenthood official who argued that President Bush's pro-life position connected him to "the Taliban's treatment of women."

We should refuse to change positions—but we also cannot be like immobile Buckingham Palace guards. We need to fight back against the libel of the *New York Times* and other publications, not because they have the power to persecute Christians but because their harassment undermines national survival. The turnaround the *Times* led after September 11 undercut the expansion of popular religious expression that followed the September 11 attacks. More people than usual were showing religious concern in small ways such as singing "God Bless America" during the seventh-inning stretch of baseball games, and in large ways as well. That limited revival fizzled as Americans heard repeatedly that strong belief is a problem, because those who have it are potential bin Ladens.

More specifically, harassment of Christians hurts the poor. Biblical conservatives have been the driving force behind compassionate conservatism, which remains our nation's best hope of helping the poor without expanding the power of government over domestic affairs—and in that way increasing opportunities for tyranny. Besides, when wars on poverty redline Christianity, they typically turn left toward soft-hearted automatic handouts or right toward hard-headed harshness. Christianity is a religion that emphasizes grace for those who repent; those who do not understand living by grace prefer a works-oriented religion where we get out of our practice exactly what we put into it. That commonly leaves most of the poor, who have not put in enough, either in passive receptivity or active frustration.

But those most hurt by harassment are the victims of persecution abroad. The one *New York Times* piece I ran across in 2002 that had words of praise for evangelicals reported this phenomenon. Nicholas Kristof wrote on May 21 that "America's evangelicals have become the newest internationalists." Kristof apparently did not realize that, due to interest in missions, they have been this way all along, but he was impressed with "evangelicals who are using their growing clout to skewer China and North Korea, to support Israel, to fight sexual trafficking in Eastern Europe and slavery in Sudan, and, increasingly, to battle AIDS in Africa." He noted that evangelical efforts led to "the International Religious Freedom Act of 1998 (fighting religious persecution) and the Trafficking Victims Protection Act of 2000 (battling sex slavery and peonage), both passed over objections of the Clinton administration."

There is a danger in concentrating attention abroad or steering Christian activity in the direction a Kristof prefers. In 1830 several Christian businessmen in New York City funded the work of John McDowell, a crusading journalist/minister. When he started writing articles about New York business practices and noting that some Christian businessmen were doing well financially by renting buildings to brothels at many times the rate they would otherwise receive, McDowell's prime backers stopped sending him contributions and began supporting William Lloyd Garrison, the famous abolitionist journalist who wrote about the evils of slavery 500 miles to the south. Fighting distant evil is good, but we should not overlook sin such as abortion in our own backyards.

Nevertheless, it's terrific that, as the Hudson Institute's Michael Horowitz wrote to evangelical leaders in May 2001, "You have led the way in making international religious liberty a major element of American foreign policy. . . . You have led the way in taking on the slavery issue of our time—the annual trafficking of millions of women and children into lives of sexual bondage. . . . You have led the way in organizing a campaign to end a growing epidemic of prison rape. . . . As you define your human rights successes as central to who you are and what you've done, it will no longer be possible for those who fear your faith to crudely caricature you or to ignore the virtue that Christian activism brings to American life and the world at large."

THE CONSISTENCY OF PRESS ATTACK

Michael Horowitz spoke too soon, for the caricaturing came back in force after September 11, and the Media Research Center in Washington, D.C., has tracked a constant stream of sneering on television network news shows in recent years. One classic statement came from NBC's Katie Couric, who began an interview by commenting on "a climate that some say has been established by religious zealots or Christian conservatives [and has led to] the dragging death of James Byrd. . . ." Christian conservatives, it seems, are Klansmen, with or without robes.

Press attacks on Christians are not a new phenomenon. At the 1925 Scopes "monkey trial" in Dayton, Tennessee, reporters regularly attacked Christian faith and "this superheated religious atmosphere, this pathetic search for the 'eternal truth.'" One journalist described John Scopes, the teacher-defendant, as an imprisoned martyr, "the witch who is to be burned by Dayton." (Actually, Scopes did not spend a second in jail and was regularly invited to dinner by Dayton Christians.) Jurors, who after the trial gave thoughtful accounts of the proceeding, gained this description in one New York headline: "Intelligence of Most of Lowest Grade." It seemed that "All twelve are Protestant churchgoers."

In recent years attitudes of and toward Christians have had a crucial political impact. During the Clinton impeachment debates of 1998, outright Clinton defenders and opponents largely balanced each other. The crucial role fell to those who did not like Mr. Clinton but hated and feared Ken Starr, the "fundamentalist" who demanded that Americans take a hard look at the facts and bring justice to a wrongdoer. Those in the middle did not take a stand but wanted to feel downright upright, and they killed the impeachment drive rather than link up with Christian conservatives.

Or look at the first part of 2000, the months of the John McCain craze among journalists. Senator McCain started out running as a moderate conservative but then, according to reporter Richard Sisk of the *New York Daily News* on March 4, became "determined to rid the GOP of big money and the Christian right influence." This was sensational because that same Christian right had been a large source of GOP volunteers and probably the Republican Party's moral center as well.

Just as comparing Scopes trial transcripts with newspaper accounts makes it clear that many reporters were describing their own prejudices rather than the actual courtroom proceedings, so do some accounts of speeches make it seem as if the speakers and reporters inhabited parallel universes. On June 11, 2002, Southern Baptist Convention (SBC) president James Merritt told the SBC's annual gathering, "We love homosexuals. God loves homosexuals. But he loves them too much to leave them homosexuals." Merritt went on to describe joyfully how two lesbians he had been talking with had become Christians, and concluded, "Christ has the power to change anybody. And so I urge you never ever condemn a blind man because he cannot see."

The Associated Press reported the address as follows: "ST. LOUIS (AP)—The head of the Southern Baptists condemned homosexuality from the podium yesterday. . . . 'Stop killing us. Stop the spiritual violence,' one [gay demonstrator] shouted. . . . 'You need Jesus,' shouted back the Rev. Robert Smith, a pastor from Cedar Bluff, Ala. Others hissed . . ." Words such as *condemned* and *hissed* convey an impression of hatred.

That story had its play and then gave way to a better example of Southern Baptist "bigotry." Rev. Jerry Vines, pastor of the First Baptist Church of Jacksonville, Florida, told the SBC gathering that "Islam was founded by Muhammad, a demon-possessed pedophile who had 12 wives—and his last one was a 9-year-old girl." This was very tough language (I prefer Merritt's pastoral emphasis), but Vines's statement arguably had a factual base. In Islam the Hadith—stories of Muhammad's life—have canonical status second only to the Quran, and the most revered collection of Hadith (the Bukhari-edited one) notes that Muhammad had many wives, including nine-year-old Aisha.

Some Muslims say Aisha was actually older, and theologians have debated for almost 1,400 years whether Muhammad was demon-possessed, but journalists should not have been shocked that Vines, a former SBC president, took a strong stand against Islam. Nor was it big news that he spoke colorfully. When a pastor is talking to other pastors and church leaders at a conference, a preach-off (something like a Pillsbury bake-off) takes place. Everyone at these conferences rolls out the rhetorical cannon. Reporters and Muslim lobbyists, though, made a big deal of Vines's statements. A *New York Times* news story on June 15 cited the remarks as an example of "hate speech against Muslims" that has "become a staple of conservative Christian political discourse." The Associated Press quoted Muslim complaints about "hate-filled and bigoted language."

Instead of attempting to determine objective facts, journalists merely emphasized subjectivity, as did a publication with an honest title, *PR Week*: The Baptist leader had uttered what "was deemed hate speech by Muslims and condemned by Jewish groups, other Christian denominations, and moderate Baptists." Vines also received support, but an Associated Press reporter emphasized hate, hate, hate, and came up with a nifty quotation from Islamic Studies professor Ingrid Mattson: The Vines statement "makes me wonder what's the hateful religion right now that we should be worried about."

The *Washington Post* on June 23, 2002, editorialized that "Some people who follow these things say no one should be surprised by the anti-Muslim bigotry of a former leader of the Southern Baptist Convention. Maybe that's right; maybe when the Rev. Jerry Vines, a former president of the convention, called the prophet Muhammad a 'demon-possessed pedophile,' we shouldn't have been shocked, only disgusted." The *Post* did not note that Vines after the preach-off stood by his analysis but tempered his tone. And in the *New York Times* on July 9, columnist Nicholas Kristof—who had praised the biblical commitment that led to international charity—called Vines's initial remarks "hate speech" and "religious bigotry." Kristof apparently did not realize that the same desire to follow the Bible underlay both what he liked and what he despised.

Attacks on Vines are also ironic given the way newspapers have typically responded to foul attacks on Christ and other biblical figures. When Christians (as discussed in chapter 1) protested the portrait of Jesus' mother, Mary, that used clumps of elephant dung and cutouts from pornographic magazines, the ever-so-sensitive *New York Times* on October 5, 1999, described the work by Chris Ofili as "witty . . . attractive . . . colorful and glowing. The first impression it makes, before you decipher the little [porn] cutouts, is that it's cheerful, even sweet." Another *Times* reporter pointed out: "While news reports have described his paintings as being splattered with dung, the clumps are actually carefully placed." Whew, that's a relief.

Similarly, when Christians in 1998 criticized Terrance McNally's play *Corpus Christi*, which portrays Jesus as a homosexual, the *Washington Post* asked, "What's wrong with letting individuals decide what they want to see?" The *Chicago Tribune* stated that "those who are uncomfortable with—or opposed to—the linking of gay themes with the narrative of the synoptic Gospels would not want to attend this particular show." The *Tribune* never said that Jerry Vines's Muhammad-criticizing comments were no big deal because those who are uncomfortable with—or opposed to—criticism of Islam would not want to attend a Southern Baptist conference.

The *New York Times* attacked Vines for offering up the "hate speech against Muslims" that has "become a staple of conservative Christian political discourse," but the *Times* did not note that *Corpus Christi* reveals that hatred of Christ and Christians is a staple of culturally liberal artists.

CHOOSING EDUCATIONAL CHOICES

Two weeks after the Vines-burning, a bigger story arrived: the Supreme Court ruling on school vouchers. After a lead sentence announcing the decision, the initial Associated Press story about *Zelman v. Simmons-Harris* continued this way: "The 5-4 ruling led by the court's conservative majority lowers the figurative wall separating church and state and clears a constitutional cloud from school vouchers, a divisive education idea dear to political conservatives and championed by President Bush. Opponents call vouchers a fraud meant to siphon tax money from struggling public schools."

Although the Associated Press in recent years has frequently given up the pretense of "neutral" journalism, words such as *divisive* and *fraud* are still pretty rough in a purportedly unbiased story—particularly because the fact pattern was summarized well by Chief Justice William Rehnquist's majority opinion: "The Ohio program is entirely neutral with respect to religion. It provides benefits directly to a wide spectrum of individuals, defined only by financial need and residence in a particular school district. It permits such individuals to exercise genuine choice among options public and private, secular and religious. The program is therefore a program of true private choice [that] does not offend the Establishment Clause."

The Associated Press labeled vouchers a "divisive idea," but Clarence Thomas's concurring opinion pointed out that the governmental educational system was already divisive. Alluding to Frederick Douglass's statement that education "means emancipation," Justice Thomas wrote, "Today many of our inner-city public schools deny emancipation to urban minority students. Despite this Court's observation nearly 50 years ago in *Brown v. Board of Education,* that 'it is doubtful that any child may reasonably be expected to succeed in life if he is denied the opportunity of an education,' urban children have been forced into a system that continually fails them."

Before even explaining what the Supreme Court majority had decided, the Associated Press had opponents calling vouchers a "fraud."

The AP story did not quote Justice Thomas's examination of the real fraud: "While in theory providing education to everyone, the quality of public schools varies significantly across districts." Nor did it quote Mr. Thomas's explanation of how prime advocates of vouchers are trying to save lives, not "siphon" funds: "Just as blacks supported public education during Reconstruction, many blacks and other minorities now support school choice programs because they provide the greatest educational opportunities for their children in struggling communities.... While the romanticized ideal of universal public education resonates with the cognoscenti who oppose vouchers, poor urban families just want the best education for their children."

The opposition to vouchers was evident on the news pages, but the editorial pages gave more reasons for the opposition. The *New York Times* editorialized about the awful situation of parents choosing "between a failing public school system and the city's parochial schools.... Not surprisingly, fully 96.6 percent of students end up taking their vouchers to religiously affiliated schools." The *Kansas City Star* praised dissenting Justice David Souter's comment that the decision by an overwhelming majority of Cleveland parents to put their children in Christian schools could not possibly reflect the genuine choice of parents. The *Los Angeles Times* argued that choice isn't necessarily bad, "but what if the choice were only between public and religious schools?"

Editorial staffs of these and other newspapers were clearly troubled at the prospect of more and more children attending Christian schools. The best way for Christians and conservatives to approach such bigotry is to focus rationally on the question at hand: The problem is not Christianity; the problem is poor education. Similarly, we should note that the problem on September 11 wasn't religious belief; the problem was murder. The problem on our highways isn't the existence of drivers; it's reckless driving. The rational way to cut highway fatalities is not to demand that everyone ride bicycles; it's to prosecute drivers who kill. The rational way to deal with bin Laden's terrorism is not to decry strong religious belief; it's to keep the murderers from murdering again.

Even though it is hard to slay bigotry, Christians are called to try. Andrew Sullivan, for example, seems to believe that the Inquisition has booths on every corner and that fundamentalists are trying to coerce others to build a world in which "sin is outlawed and punished and constantly purged—by force if necessary." But he evidently doesn't understand that Christianity is based on belief, not rites, and belief can't be forced. Nor does he recognize the way revelation and reason go together, and the deep respect Christians have for conscience. He doesn't seem to understand the basic Christian teaching that man cannot outlaw sin and build walls against it because sin comes from within.

Sullivan and others view free religious faith as impossible unless politics and religion are totally separated; yet such a separation is logically impossible. That's because all political positions are based in views that some things are good and evil—and those are religious characterizations. As Don Feder, an Orthodox Jewish syndicated columnist, has explained, "It's said *the religious right* wants to force its faith on the public. But whose faith are we talking about? [Every group] in the political arena wants to see their morals reflected in our laws and governmental institutions—including the National Organization of Women, the National Abortion Rights Action League, and the American Civil Liberties Union, whether or not they are willing to admit it."

Christians should not be unduly bothered by attacks. As the apostle James wrote at the beginning of his epistle, "Consider it pure joy, my brothers, whenever you face trials of many kinds, because you know that the testing of your faith develops perseverance" (Jas. 1:2-3 NIV). But the "why" question about journalistic biases remains even after the who, what, when, where, and how questions fade. Why, with so many bad guys to go after, do many leading journalists train their guns on Christians who, for the most part, tend to turn the other cheek?

IGNORANCE OR MALICE?

Christian parents who raise boys learn the question to ask when meditating on the proper punishment for a transgression: "Is it boy, or is it sin?" Boy nature, impetuous and adventuresome, can get young males into trouble. Parents need to help their charges become more responsible but should not assume the malice of sin unless direct disobedience is evident. The Christian response to secular liberal reporters should be similar: "Is it ignorance or malice?"

Some observers contend that journalists are not so much biased against Christianity as ignorant of it. One study commissioned by the First Amendment Center at Vanderbilt University contended that journalists should "take religion seriously," and journalism students should "include at least one religion course" in their programs of study. This Gannett-funded center responded to accusations of bias by plea-bargaining: There is "more ignorance about religion than bias in the average newsroom."

Journalistic ignorance is certainly apparent in the common depiction of fundamentalists as uneducated folks. Fundamentalist leaders early in the last century included erudite theologians who adhered to creeds and statements such as those of the Niagara Bible Conference of 1878 and the Presbyterian General Assembly of 1910. The twelve volumes of essays ("the Fundamentals") written from 1910 to 1915 by sixty-four British and American ministers and theologians are highly literate documents. The essays thoughtfully contend that the Bible is inspired by God and that strict but not unthinking or unreasonable adherence to its teachings makes great sense.

Today American fundamentalists range from the unschooled to the highly literate. Scholars today know that "fundamentalist" is not a particularly useful definer. As Fred M. Donner, chairman of the Department of Near Eastern Languages and Civilizations at the University of Chicago, told one reporter, "The word 'fundamentalist' tends to be a pejorative. There are dozens of different kinds. Some are very pacifistic, some are very unpacifistic. They disagree among themselves. To condemn people as fundamentalists is painting with a broad brush." But some professors teach condemnation, or at least fear of fundamentalists. A decade ago, the Williamsburg Charter Survey on Religion and Public Life found that 92 percent of surveyed academics were worried that evangelicals were trying to merge church and state. One-third even claimed that evangelicals (an even broader category than fundamentalists) were "a threat to democracy."

That is not useful Shimei criticism; such fear shows ignorance. American Christians have not had to receive instruction from the outside about separating church and state because that division is biblical. Moses was the lawgiver, Aaron the priest. Saul was king; Samuel was prophet. Ahab tried to become a dictator; Elijah opposed him. Representatives of both priesthood and kingdom, each assigned to keep the other honest, watched over contributions to the temple building fund. Much later, when Christians had political power in Europe, popes and emperors or bishops and kings checked and sometimes balanced each other. The U.S. Constitution, with its emphasis on checks and balances, is based on the concept that sin lurks within us all; so power must be divided, and all must be watched.

Did churches in ancient and medieval times sometimes overstep their bounds? Of course, but defining Christianity in terms of the sins that have been committed in its name is like defining electricity solely as that which made the electric chair. The key question in American society is not whether church will overawe state but whether the state will deprive Christians of the freedom to criticize what the Bible says is sin. Will media and governmental leaders accept a diversity of opinion and tolerate those who say what God has said, or will any such comments be labeled Talibanesque "hate speech"? The prosecutor is standing by.

Is it sin or is it boy? Among journalists, is misreporting of Christians ignorance, or is it malice? Most journalists who have grown up in nonbiblical homes will naturally see people with biblical perspectives as weird and will report from some combination of ignorance and malice. But in my experience, patient explanation can at least educate some reporters to the point where they realize that they can begin to think logically about Christianity. Some may even begin to see that beyond either ignorance or malice lies a third factor: fear.

CHRISTOPHOBIA OR EGOMANIA?

We live in an age of phobias. These days when we turn tail and run, we are no longer supposed to admit that we are cowards; we say we are merely acting in accord with our phobias. The Bible describes a true phobia—fear of God and His angels—that truly is a consuming fire for many. Almost every angel in the Bible needed to say to men and women quivering in the presence of the supernatural, "Fear not." That's because we are all sinners and have good reason to fear a holy God until He graciously tells us, "Fear not," and even more graciously provides a way to escape His wrath. If we run from Christ, we fear Him all the more because deep down we know we are throwing away our only realistic hope.

Christophobia, unlike homophobia, receives little press coverage. The Lexis Nexis online archive has averaged only one reference to Christophobia per year over the past twenty years, but over 1,000 references in each recent year to homophobia. From talking with many Washington reporters who came to Austin in 1999 to find out about George W. Bush, my sense is that Christophobia is rampant among them. Many fear a loss of autonomy and even a loss of the cynicism that allows them to feel intellectually superior to others. Christophobia even makes some snap at allies. The *New Republic*, a strong journalistic supporter of Israel, attacked evangelical supporters of Israel because the support offered was "Messianic," based in the hope that more Jews will become Christians. "If you don't love Israel for what it is, you can't be trusted to love it at all." *New York Times* columnist Frank Rich even announced that he was "paranoid" about Christians since the helpful things evangelicals do arise from "theological self-interest" in proclaiming Christ.

I also saw a lot of egocentrism, and some journalists admit it. It's reflected in the continuing popularity of J. D. Salinger's novel *The Catcher in the Rye,* a favorite of many journalists. The book's central figure—deeply alienated prep school student Holden Caulfield—and its reclusive author have had a cult following for decades. Mark Chapman had a copy when he shot John Lennon. In the movie *Conspiracy Theory,* the semi-hinged character played by Mel Gibson had to buy up every copy he saw. The book even made the Modern Library's list of the hundred best novels of the twentieth century.

For those worshiping the teenager's trinity of me, myself, and I, Holden Caulfield's half-crazy emphasis on living his erratic feelings from moment to moment, along with his utter contempt for the "phony" people and social structures surrounding him, has been enormously appealing. Holden lives out the pessimistic parts of Ecclesiastes: "I have seen all the things that are done under the sun; all of them are meaningless, a chasing after the wind"(Eccl. 1:14 NIV). Sad to say, Caufield does not perceive the distinction in Ecclesiastes between things done "under the sun" and things done through Christ. He wants to be a catcher in the rye. He imagines himself standing by a cliff and keeping kids playing in a rye field nearby from falling off. And yet he needs a catcher himself.

I've seen among many journalists Caulfield's idealism and cynicism—wanting to be a catcher in the rye, constantly seeing "phonies," and in the process becoming phony themselves. Many had largely absentee fathers. New York University psychologist Paul Vitz has researched the history of intellectuals who felt let down by their fathers on earth and thereafter mocked those who had faith in a Father in heaven. My impressionistic sense is that the same tendency can be found among many leading journalists.

Many of these journalists are also believers in progressive history. Their patron saint could be H. G. Wells, who a century ago wrote not only science fiction but also *The Outline of History,* which portrayed mankind "at first scattered and blind and utterly confused, feeling its way slowly to the serenity and salvation of an ordered and coherent purpose." That purpose was a world government strong enough to bring about "harmonious cooperation" that would leave behind "narrow, selfish, and contradicting nationalist traditions." Wells and other progressives laid out a process of social salvation that was also individually aggrandizing.

Since Wells posited the absence of God, man has no hope of eternal life, but in this life he is autonomous and able to change the flow of history through decisions that transcend earlier understandings of right and wrong. Wellsian history goes well with the work of Lawrence Kohlberg, known in schools of education for his theory of ethical stages through which people progress: from following the law to "social duty" and ultimately to "autonomous ethical thinking," where a person makes up his own principles. Kohlberg argued that such ethical autonomy should be the goal of human existence, even though at this stage humans are in some ways the most selfish, virtually inventing a world totally apart from God.

The journalism students and journalists I've talked with over the past several years expressed faith in their own autonomous judgment. One typical reporter's response was, "I make my decisions based on what I feel is right." Another journalist said he affirmed some Christian principles, but "the bottom line is, I believe in me." A third said, "My governing belief is, the only person you can really trust in life is yourself." A fourth believed in "taking bits and pieces from several religions and in that way making up my own, personal religion."

I've also had the opportunity to talk with some religion editors and reporters at major newspapers. They also commonly tilt toward autonomy, praising (as the *Washington Post* did in 2001) those who "write their own Bible. They fashion their own God . . . turning him into a social planner, therapist or guardian angel." The *Post* told the story of Ed and Joanne Liverani, who decided to "build their own church, salvaging bits of their old religion they liked and chucking the rest." They ended up with a god who "cheers them up when they're sad, laughs at their quirks." Lynn Garrett, a religious book tracker for *Publishers Weekly*, called this "an eclectic approach. People borrow ideas from different traditions, then add them to whatever religion they're used to." As the *Washington Post* noted, having a "self-made deity" is popular now, particularly among journalists.

Faith in God logically requires assent to the proposition that God is wiser than we are. Long ago Augustine said, "If you believe in the gospel what you like, and reject what you don't like, it is not the gospel you believe, but yourself." The *New York Times* portrayed Steven Weinberg, a Nobel Prize-winning theoretical physicist, musing, "Even if there is a God, how do you know that his moral judgments are the correct ones? Seems to me Abraham should have said, 'God, that's just not right.'" Weinberg is brilliant, but if God is limited to judgments with which only a very bright person agrees, then God can be no more discerning than that person. A god only as smart as the Liveranis or even Steven Weinberg would not be much of a god to follow.

Deep down, adherents to the religion of self always worry that the real God will show up. As even Ted Koppel pointed out, it doesn't make sense for the Ten Commandments to become the Ten Suggestions. If they really come from God, we should follow them. Mockers know that. Cafeteria-style Christianity, with every person told to pick what he or she wants to follow and disregard the rest, is the opposite extreme from legalism but may be its illegitimate son. When parents tell children, "Do not touch anything," kids are not taught to distinguish among different activities and may rebelliously end up touching everything.

Instead of emulating the Liveranis and pressing on to Kohlberg's seventh and highest stage, "autonomous ethical thinking," I suggest three stages of movement. The first and lowest is purported autonomy, better known as I'm-the-center-of-the-world self-glorification stage. The second stage is where we are loyal to something outside of and bigger than ourselves, perhaps a nation, perhaps a concept. The real hope is to move by grace to the highest stage where we act to bring glory to God the Creator and not to ourselves or other creatures (although in the course of glorifying God, we may bring honor to ourselves and to our nation or business).

Progress through these stages is not easy, and the motives of even those God has claimed remain mixed. But what Holden Caulfield needed was not a vision of himself as the catcher in the rye but a biblical vision. Then Holden would know that Christ is the catcher.

3

RESPONDING TO
IGNORANCE

Biblically, when we are attacked verbally, we are not to assume malice. The aggressor may be ill-informed, or he may be so frightened of us and what we represent that he sees his choices as fight or flight, and he chooses to lash out. This "judgment of charity" suggests that without proof we should not assume the presence of evil. Charity toward journalists means that we interpret bias not necessarily as malice but as ignorance and fear. In response, we should provide information and the biblical imperative, "Fear not." We should then pray for God to work in the hearts of men and women.

I've seen three particular areas of journalistic ignorance: the current extent of adherence to Christianity in the world, the historical relationship of Christians and government in America, and the cultural and philanthropic activities of many Christians today. The first gap is factually easy to fill. Although many reporters write as if Christianity is a Western religion and is declining as Europe fades both in population and power, the number of people identifying with Christianity increased from 588 million in 1900 to two billion in 2000, with growth almost entirely in less-developed nations. In these nations, the number of adherents grew from 83 million to 1.12 billion. Specifically, the number of adherents to Christianity in Africa grew thirty-eight-fold; adherence to Islam impressively grew tenfold during the century, but Christians now outnumber Muslims in Africa.

In 1900 some 81 percent of Christians were white, and that dropped to 45 percent in 2000, according to David Barrett's *World Christian Encyclopedia*. On a typical Sunday probably more believers attend church in China than in all of purportedly Christian Europe. More Anglicans attend church in each of these five African countries—Nigeria, Kenya, South Africa, Tanzania, and Uganda—than do Anglicans in the United Kingdom and Episcopalians in the United States combined. More Presbyterians are in church in Ghana than in Scotland, more in South Africa than in the United States. More members of the Assemblies of God are in church in Brazil than in the United States.

TWO CENTURIES OF CHRISTIAN INTERACTION WITH GOVERNMENT

The lack of knowledge about Christianity around the world is exceeded only by an inaccurate understanding of its past in America. Andrew Sullivan wrote in the *New York Times* on October 7, 2001, that "American evangelicalism has always kept its distance from governmental power" until recently when "the temptation to fuse political and religious authority beckoned more insistently." That's nonsense. Evangelicals have always been politically involved. They changed America through the agitation that led up to the American Revolution, through their sustained pressure to abolish slavery, and through many other attempts to merge religious and governmental concerns.

Many secular journalists don't see this because they have been educated as materialists, believing that the key reasons people and societies change are economic. Let's look at the highlights of the religion-politics connection since Colonial days, beginning with how the Great Awakening changed many individuals and led to a decreased distinction between religious and political activities. Even a minister as theologically centered as Jonathan Edwards told New Englanders that they should compare good officials with those "contemptible" ones who are "of a mean spirit, a disposition that will admit of their doing those things that are sordid and vile." Such appointees "will shamefully . . . screw their neighbours, and will take advantage of their authority or commission to line their own pockets with what is fraudulently taken or withheld from others."

Evangelists such as Gilbert Tennett were careful to insist that Christians are "born for Society" and must work for "the Good of the Publick, which we were born to promote." Minister Benjamin Lord noted in 1751 that the colonists were "Prone to act in Civil, as they stand Affected in religious Matters." The signing of a certain political petition could become "a Sabbath-Day's Exercise," and churches sometimes voted as blocs. Leading ministers urged their listeners to leave corrupt churches and work against a corrupt government.

Patrick Henry's famous pre-Revolution speech used biblical language to decry gentlemen who cried "'peace, peace'—but there is no peace." With Virginia facing a British Nebuchadnezzar to the north, Henry suggested that the colony would go the way of ancient Judea unless its people were bold and courageous. "Why stand we here idle?" he asked. "Is life so dear, or peace so sweet, as to be purchased at the price of chains and slavery?" Henry answered, "Forbid it, Almighty God! I know not what course others may take; but as for me, give me liberty, or give me death!" Henry then brought his biblical sensibility directly into politics as he became governor of Virginia.

Henry's Massachusetts counterpart Samuel Adams did the same 500 miles to the north, using biblical language and references to explain to his countrymen the significance of their battle with Britain. Adams began his *First Book of the American Chronicles of the Times* with a description of how "the Bostonites arose a great multitude, and destroyed the TEA, the abominable merchandise of the east, and cast it into the midst of the sea." In Adams's parody of Old Testament lists of nations (Hittites, Jebusites, etc.), the New Yorkites, Virginites, Carolinites, and others, uniting in a refusal to worship the "Tea Chest

Idol," became Americanites, "and the ears of all the people hearkened unto the book of the law."

Early state constitutions emphasized reverence for God along with a separation of denomination and state. Maryland's constitution proclaimed that "it is the duty of every man to worship God in such manner as he thinks most acceptable to him." Crucially, there would be no established denomination; no one would "be compelled to frequent or maintain, or contribute, unless on contract, to maintain any particular place of worship, or any particular ministry." The South Carolina constitution had no proscription on taxes supporting churches as long as no one was "obliged to pay towards the maintenance and support of a religious worship" not his own.

The Massachusetts constitution of 1780 specified, "It is the right as well as the Duty of all men in society, publicly and at stated seasons to worship the Supreme Being, the great Creator and preserver of the Universe." These New Englanders of the Revolution were different from their Puritan forebears, but they still saw religious belief as essential. The new state constitution declared that "The happiness of a people, and the good order and preservation of civil government, essentially depend upon piety, religion, and morality. . . . these cannot be generally diffused through a Community, but by the institution of the public worship of God, and of public instructions in piety, religion, and morality."

The First Amendment to the U.S. Constitution came into being to provide freedom *for* religion, not freedom *from* religion—but that is an oft-told tale. Less known is how nineteenth-century leaders of all kinds, including Supreme Court justices and evangelist Charles Finney, united in stressing the need for a religious base in politics. Finney, active from the 1820s through the 1870s and often portrayed as concerned only about heaven, stressed that "the time has come for Christians to *vote for honest men*, and take consistent ground in politics, or the Lord will curse them."

Alexis de Tocqueville noted in the 1830s that "Americans combine the notions of Christianity and of liberty so intimately in their minds that it is impossible to make them conceive the one without the other." Tocqueville and others were not saying that the United States had a church-state union similar to that of Muslim states now, but a Christianity-liberty union. Biblical Christianity promoted a sense of "the priesthood of all believers," so that all could read the Bible and freely develop their own consciousness of right and wrong, along with the willingness to stand up for their beliefs.

Many presidents also were heavily influenced by their evangelical beliefs and did not try to hide that fact. Andrew Jackson is not generally known as one of our most religious presidents, but in 1832 he vetoed a bill to recharter the influence-peddling, economy-centralizing Second Bank of the United States. Jackson wrote, "In the full enjoyment of the gifts of Heaven and the fruit of superior industry, economy, and virtue, every man is equally entitled to protection by law." Even when the U.S. Senate censured him, Jackson held firm in his Bible-based understanding—"I will not bow down to the golden calf"—and eventually won.

In the late nineteenth century Grover Cleveland fought both political and theological liberalism, maintaining that "the Bible is good enough for me" and that "criticism, or explanations about authorship or origin" was irrelevant. He argued that abandonment of the gold standard would lead to inflation and injure "the laborer or workingman, as he sees the money he has received for his toil shrink and shrivel in his hand." Pro-inflation leader William Jennings Bryan called Cleveland a Pontius Pilate and melded his own theology with populist politics as he accepted the 1896 Democratic presidential nomination: "You shall not press down upon the brow of labor this crown of thorns. You shall not crucify mankind upon a cross of gold."

Early in the twentieth century Theodore Roosevelt gave speeches and published articles with explicit titles such as "The Eighth and Ninth Commandments in Politics." He described how any kind of

economic preferment because of political ties "comes dangerously
near the border-line of the commandment which, in forbidding
theft, certainly by implication forbids the connivance at theft, or the
failure to punish it." He insisted that government-mandated economic redistribution might be politically popular, but the leader who
appealed to covetousness "is not, and never can be, aught but an
enemy of the very people he professes to befriend. . . . To break the
Tenth Commandment is no more moral now than it has been for the
past thirty centuries."

Cynical observers such as British writer John Morley hated
Roosevelt's combination of whirligig-speaking style and scriptural
quotations. He called Roosevelt a combination of "St. Paul and St.
Vitus," and Speaker of the House Thomas B. Reed sarcastically con-
gratulated Roosevelt on his "original discovery of the Ten
Commandments." But Roosevelt persisted in his linking of Bible and
politics and insisted on clear and concrete applications of biblical
commandments. He often noted, "The Eighth Commandment
reads: 'Thou shall not steal.' It does not read: 'Thou shall not steal
from the rich man.' It does not read: 'Thou shall not steal from the
poor man.' It reads simply and plainly: 'Thou shall not steal.'"*

Roosevelt, in short, sounded like what today would be called a
fundamentalist, and so did many other presidents and many leaders
of popular movements. For example, religious belief animated both
the mid-nineteenth-century and mid-twentieth-century drives for
racial fairness. Civil rights leaders weren't out to subvert American
democracy; nor are devout activists today. They claimed and claim an
inalienable right to defend rights not granted by people (who may
choose to take them away) but granted by God (who does not
change). Journalists who miss this don't know enough about the
American past to weigh in thoughtfully about the American future.

---

*These quotations and others from Jackson, Cleveland, and Roosevelt may be found
in my book *The American Leadership Tradition* (The Free Press, 1999).

Nor do many journalists know much about contemporary American Christianity and the impact of belief on those who have overcome Christophobia. Look, for example, at what Christianity did to Kurt Warner, who came from athletic exile in Europe to the Most Valuable Player awards in the National Football League in 1999 and 2001.

For a star like that, with a new seven-year, $46-million contract, time truly is money. He can rake in big bucks for appearing in ads, and he can also do his bit for charity by appearing in a United Way commercial. What he will not offer, unless he's unusual, is challenging, personal, and spiritual help directly to those in need. Who has the time? Who needs the aggravation? But Warner, along with giving money to his First Things First Foundation and to charities such as Camp Barnabas (a Christian retreat in Missouri for special-needs children), also gives his time.

He's given Sunshine Ministries, a homeless shelter in St. Louis, twenty tickets to each home game so that impoverished men, women, and teens have a chance to see him in action. That's good but not hard for a multimillionaire. What's striking is that Warner takes the twenty ticket recipients out to dinner on Fridays before the games. Warner, his wife, Barbara, and their four children sit with their guests around a big table.

One week a New York Giants fan was among the homeless guys at dinner; so Warner took him on, joking back and forth about the Giants and Warner's St. Louis Rams. They continued the repartee for weeks. Carol Clarkson, Sunshine's program director, says "the guys feel special" to be eating with the MVP, "but he's so natural with us that they get comfortable with him. And he remembers the guys." Warner also takes his guests with him to services at the St. Louis Family Church. Call the ACLU!

Kurt Warner came from a modest religious interest to evangelical enthusiasm. He came from being fancy-free to marrying a woman with two young children from a previous marriage, one of whom is legally blind. He came from modest success as a high school quarterback and lots of bench-sitting at Northern Iowa University, hardly known as a National Football League feeder school. He came from working at a supermarket for $5.50 per hour when he couldn't get a football job. Mrs. Clarkson says, "The important thing is that Kurt knows where he came from, and he hasn't forgotten it."

Journalists these days always watch for religious hypocrisy. Mr. Warner talks frequently about being a Christian, and if he indulged in trash-talking and showboating or appeared arrogant, reporters would be on the attack. They're not. *Sports Illustrated* writers have left behind any gee-whiz attitudes towards stars; so it's significant that an *SI* profile on October 18, 1999, observed, "The more you watch Warner interact with his family—and reaffirm his faith—the less stunning his phenomenal ascent seems. He appears to be sincere, unabashed and unspoiled."

That's unusual—but reporters haven't written much about why that is. They have written about Warner's work ethic. After the Rams gave him a backup job, he practiced and practiced, was ready when their starter was injured early in the 1999 season, and led the team to a Super Bowl victory. But they haven't figured out why Warner helps the poor in a way that challenges them to do better, and how Warner knows that to "love your neighbor as yourself" means pushing that neighbor to work hard. Reporters are missing a good story.

THE CASE OF JOHN SMOLTZ

In 1996 many sports sections covered the purported psychological change in one of baseball's best pitchers, John Smoltz. Smoltz, who won that year the Cy Young Award as the National League's best pitcher, says he had "gone to a sports psychologist, but that whole story was hyped. It kept going and going, and writers kept writing it without ever asking me about it. . . . The real change is that in 1996 I began to understand that apart from Christ, we can do nothing. I started to have a peace about things."

Arm trouble followed in the next several years, as Smoltz recalled while standing in front of his locker in the Atlanta Braves clubhouse on July 4, 2002: "God started stripping me of my control. My arm went. . . . A lot of people have faith in the process until the process fails us. That's what I faced." Speaking intensely, he gestured around the clubhouse and said, "Baseball was God to me. It's God to most of the people here. But this last year has been the greatest challenge and the greatest blessing. . . . I realized I don't need baseball. I've gained total confidence that God is in control. No more fear."

That sense of liberation produced results on the field but, even more importantly, off it. Smoltz began pitching well again late in 2001, but he said his happiest day that year came "when I walked in and saw our school opening. I almost broke down . . . through Christ, we overcome so much." That school is King's Ridge Christian School, which exists in Atlanta's northern suburbs largely because Smoltz, unable to pitch in 2000, poured himself into an education project. "Building a school takes an incredible amount of time. In one sense, I'd rather have another surgery on my arm than go through all this again."

Hiring teachers, developing curriculum, enrolling students, finding a place to meet—all very hard but "very rewarding," according to Smoltz, the father of four children, "especially when I see how God brings good out of bad." The pitcher's enthusiasm and leadership were key, according to the King's Ridge Christian School headmaster and board chairman. Meanwhile, Smoltz's excellent pitching late in 2001 led the New York Yankees to offer him a $52 million contract to work up. He almost signed, but wanting to stay in Atlanta and see his school develop, re-signed with the Braves for $30 million over three years.

While Smoltz and I talked on July 4, television sets in the Atlanta clubhouse were turned to CNN (the Braves, after all, are owned by AOL Time Warner), and the big story was of an airport shooting. Braves left fielder Chipper Jones grimaced and said, "It's happening everywhere," and that prompted Mr. Smoltz to explain passionately why Christian education should not emphasize only warm fuzzies: "Columbine—how does that happen? The girl dying because she professed her faith. . . . We want to prepare kids for battles in life. Kids need the ability to differentiate between evolution and Christian understanding. . . . They need the weapons to defend Christianity, to be able to understand and debate the differences between religions, to know what's happening in the world and how to compete."

Smoltz explained that he expected to contribute substantially to the school in money and time over the next several years, but had already received more than he could ever repay. He said he had learned to "live without fear. Now I know that whether I win or lose, God loves me just the same. Doesn't mean I won't put all my effort into the pitch—God wants us to compete, hard. But being a baseball player is not who I am; it's a product of who I am, so I don't have to worry about losing my identity. Without fear of losing, I can concentrate all my attention on the moment."

WITHOUT FEAR: GROWING SMALLER BUT DEEPER

How else does Christianity make a difference? Some publicists talk about the existence of homeless shelters; yet more important than the shelters themselves is the way Christians view people who come for help—as human beings, not pets. They see themselves as fishers of men, not feeders of subhumans.

Linda Lipa works at Sunshine Ministries, Kurt Warner's charity, and remembers handing out turkey baskets to all comers before Thanksgiving: "Some people lined up to get a turkey, then went to gas stations and sold them for drug money. Now people have to be in the program and attending weekly classes for three months to get a turkey. That has dramatically reduced the numbers, but it's more effective."

Herb Lusk, pastor of a large inner-city Philadelphia church, hands out Thanksgiving turkeys to the needy only in conjunction with a worship service and other church activities. Many other programs also have changed. When we do not see people as made in God's image, we can put food in bowls and feel we've done our duty. When we know that God reigns, the stakes are higher. In 1989, secular liberals used the word *compassion* to promote governmental spending. In 1999, some on the left still use it that way, and some on the right still scorn the word as one suggesting weak sentimentalism, but compassion has in part been reclaimed as a biblical expression that can pump iron.

Look at the transforming power in the heart of liberalism, New York City's upper west side, home of Broadway Presbyterian Church on 114th Street at Broadway. The church had established a massive feeding program for homeless folks, but some of those involved in poverty-fighting faced reality and rethought their methods. Executive director Chris Fay in 2001 recalled Broadway Community, Inc.'s founding nine years earlier: "I was working with the poor and was burnt out. We saw the same people coming for food, year after year. We saw very few breakthroughs. The people who volunteered for the soup kitchen didn't know anything about the individuals who ate there. We were doing it to feel better about ourselves."

BCI now offers effective compassion rather than guilt relief for the affluent. Participants gain clerical skills and basic computer literacy, prepare for food service and security jobs, and work in BCI micro-enterprises such as StreetSmart, a mall-cleaning group. Employees have monthly contracts and frequent evaluations. Since local employers value the judgment of BCI instructors, BCI can offer guaranteed job placements for program graduates. Graduates need to show uninterrupted sobriety and reconciliation with their families. Aware of how easy it is to lapse, BCI requires random drug testing and training in how to identify and fight habits that lead to lost jobs.

The challenge to work and the policing of behavior are too much for most people who start the program. Fay notes that participants' average age is forty, and they've been using drugs for twenty-five years. He adds, "They won't work until they've lost everything and have no alternative." But three out of five of those who stick it out for a month graduate because they can achieve much once they get their minds in gear. Fay says, "I rarely meet anybody who is incapable of working. Many have gotten used to government funding: They have no work emphasis and no purpose in life."

The job training could be dismissed by some as merely more social gospel, but the striking change over the past ten years has been the return of Christian witness. A decade ago there was practically none. Fay notes, "We even argued about whether to give thanks at meals. Union Seminary students were the biggest opponents. They said the clients would resent it." The reality was exactly the opposite. "When we did start, the clients responded, 'We never understood why you weren't saying grace.' They wondered whether we were embarrassed by Christ."

Sitting in on one discussion among clients, I saw how the new teaching was sinking in. Participants spoke of their own sinful tendencies. One woman said, "I always had to be in the driver's seat. But now I've learned that what's good to me isn't good for me." A man said, "It's not what we *want* to do that's important; it's what we *have* to do." God was becoming central in their thoughts. One woman said, "I write a note to God every night saying, 'Thank You, God, for giving me another day.'" The others backed up staff member Moira Ahearne's contention that "the clients like talking about Jesus. We [staffers] are the ones who were confused."

WITHOUT FEAR: EMPHASIZING ONE NEIGHBORHOOD

Government projects want gaudy numbers; Christian projects can proceed without fear and work intensively to change the lives of a few. For example, the Texas group Voice of Hope decided to claim only nine blocks of west Dallas for its makeover opportunity—but it really worked that area. Lawndale Community Church in Chicago took a small chunk of the city and worked to improve it, even to the extent of color-coding aerial photographs of the terrain so that no tenement goes unnoted.

Government money during recent decades has sometimes poured, sometimes trickled into North Lawndale, and the area is still one of the poorest in America. But as I walked near the church with Wayne Gordon, the man who was God's instrument in getting it going twenty-two years ago, the benefit of targeting one small area and sticking with it was apparent.

Gordon, a white graduate of Wheaton College in one of Chicago's affluent suburbs, moved to almost entirely black North Lawndale in 1975 as a coach and history teacher at Farragut High School. That sounds like a radical choice, but God prepares people for what He calls them to, and that's how it worked here. Even as a child, Wayne wanted to help poor black kids, and as a college student he volunteered at the notorious Cabrini Green housing project. When Gordon and his new bride, Ann, started a Bible study for high school kids that turned into a church, they stuck with it, even after their apartment was broken into ten times during their first three years together in North Lawndale. The church now has 500 worshiping families and a variety of programs—Hope House, Lazarus House—for men coming out of addiction or prison.

Gordon was the founding president of the Lawndale Christian Development Corporation (LCDC), which rehabs abandoned housing and has helped more than 100 families to buy homes. He helped to found the Lawndale Christian Health Center and similar organizations for dental and vision care. He has been instrumental in setting up sports programs and a computer lab for kids. The variety of programs is impressive, but their proximity to each other is key. Programs are all in a two-block area with mauve banners fluttering overhead proclaiming Lawndale Community. And that's important: We talk these days of "virtual communities" via the Internet, but building an authentic community is difficult without common geography and the people within a community seeing each other daily or at least weekly.

Proximity allows a pastor to cover his pasture. Mr. Gordon is a

shepherd who knows and hugs his sheep. As he walks his neighborhood, he hails most folks by name and asks a question related to their
activities. He learns how they're doing, and they see that he cares. Just
as the television program *Cheers* celebrated a Boston bar "where
everyone knows your name," so people rich and poor alike tend to
look for a community of caring. Developing one may require thinking small rather than big, parish rather than metropolis. In a society
that venerates size and numbers, emphasizing depth rather than
mere breadth is a radical notion.

WITHOUT FEAR: WORKING TOWARD
ALL-AROUND HEALTH

The same logic should animate our thinking about health care among
the poor. Why not work on expanding and replicating Good
Samaritan Health Services in Tulsa (Oklahoma) and its equivalents
in many cities around the country? Good Samaritan is a free clinic in
low-income north Tulsa and the sections surrounding Peoria Avenue
and 61st Street. It provides not only health care but also builds rela-
tionships that allow for the treatment of psychological, social, and
spiritual needs. Good Samaritan volunteer teams of doctors, nurses,
social workers, and other professionals provide quality primary care,
physical examinations and health screenings, vision and hearing
assessments, mental health counseling, and treatment of sexually
transmitted diseases.

The poor gain at least as much medical help as they would
through a governmental program, but to the volunteers they are persons, not numbers. More doctors willing to volunteer part of their
time are coming, and the Hillcrest Medical Center in Tulsa is offering a family-practice residency that will train more doctors in community care from a biblical perspective. A thirty-four-foot mobile
medical unit allows Good Samaritan to reach people who wouldn't
step into a doctor's office until reaching the point of utter desperation.

Internationally, Christian organizations are also working to improve health, and they often find that transforming cultures is essential to the process. The Christian development agency World Vision tells of introducing a village to agricultural innovations that could double the yield of sorghum. Its experts explained to the villagers everything the experts thought was scientifically relevant: the seeds, the chemical content of the fertilizer, and so on. Most of the villagers hesitated, but one farmer plunged ahead. He planted the seeds and showed the increased yield. World Vision folks rejoiced: Now the rest of the farmers would follow the example of the successful innovator.

It did not work out that way. The farmer's son, sad to say, died within a year. Infant mortality is 20 percent in that culture, and so such a death was not unusual. But other villagers connected the child's death with the increased crop. They concluded that the World Vision experts were offering a useful form of witchcraft, but sacrificing a son to improve yields was too high a price to pay.

Experts also learned more about the role of theology in development when they analyzed the problems of a village with huts that had only little holes in their walls. When villagers lit small fires in their huts for cooking and heating, smoke was trapped inside; eye and lung problems ensued. Development experts came, explained that the villagers needed ventilation and light, and offered to put in windows. The villagers agreed.

Three weeks later, however, the little holes were back, and the windows were gone. The villagers understood that their small holes led to poor physical health, but they had thought through the spiritual consequence of having big windows. Evil spirits would come in. The price of protection against spirits was bad health, and it was a price the villagers decided to pay. Plus, they were happy to have free windows that they could then remove and sell to people in other villages who were foolish enough to risk spiritual damage. Fear can sabotage well-laid plans, and that's why organizations are realizing that development experts and missionaries need to work side by side.

WITHOUT FEAR: LIVING IN AMERICA'S "WORST" CITIES

Money magazine in 2001 unveiled its list of "best places to live," a ranking of 328 cities using measuring rods such as job availability, crime rate, and so on. The bottom four were Memphis, TN; Albuquerque, NM; San Francisco, CA; and, in 328th place, Miami, FL. Most people would look to the top of the list—but the Bible suggests a different path. God made Jonah go to Nineveh, a city that in his day was probably the worst in the world. Two millennia ago, God became flesh, with all the indignities of being a baby; that's at least like a human choosing to be a cockroach. As a man, Christ didn't go where the living was easy, but chose to eat with and confront sinners.

Some Christians have done the same, choosing to work in challenging places. In #325 Memphis, sixty-nine-year-old Jo Walt is a southern gentlewoman who once "lived a very sheltered life." When she set up a school in a middle-class black area, some of her friends said, "I just don't do that part of the city." They were even more surprised in 1993 when she founded The Neighborhood School in the very poor Binghamton neighborhood. The school now gives 110 kindergarten through eighth grade students—including Sudanese refugee children—a Christian education. The generally absent dads of students often have drug and criminal backgrounds, and the moms are often very depressed.

Is core Memphis a good or bad place in which to live and work? "It's not a safe city," Mrs. Walt said. "It has an incredible number of homicides. You do have to be careful. We've personally had a number of robberies—but everyone has to be careful nowadays," she added, referring to the events of September 11. Moving from city #325 or restricting herself to the affluent parts of it is not an option for her: "This is just where I am. I can't imagine being anywhere else. I know what the problems are. I can't solve them all. I can [help] two or three children."

In #326 Albuquerque, Jeremy Reynalds has run Joy Junction since 1986, when he founded what has become New Mexico's largest emergency homeless shelter. Six thousand people, mostly women and children, stayed each year in the 150-bed building located immediately south of the city's sewage treatment plant. Critics call the shelter a place merely for human sewage treatment, but Joy's "Christ in Power" program, a life skills training course, has more than 100 participants each year. Sewage does not soar, as some formerly despondent humans have.

Reynalds is not surprised by the #326 ranking, since Albuquerque's crime rate is high and its unemployment above average. But he remembers a husband and wife with two small children who ended up at Joy Junction when the husband lost the job that had brought him to Albuquerque. The shelter helped husband and wife to move from spiritual hopelessness to Christianity and soon leave behind material hopelessness as well. Multiply that story many times, and Reynalds considers Albuquerque a great place to live.

In #327 San Francisco, Alpha Pregnancy Center director Donna McIlhenny encounters a city that calls itself tolerant and yet "is meanly intolerant of biblical Christianity." Her pro-life center has been defamed often in the press and spray-painted many times with slogans such as, "Get your Bible off my body," and others that are too obscene to print. "We have no political support here in the city," she says; so pro-abortion forces "can do whatever they want to us with impunity." But at Alpha volunteers give many hours of their time to help those who would otherwise sense no alternative to doing what they really do not want to do. Sometimes there are victories; one Chinese couple that planned an abortion ended up giving birth to twins, and the center was able to provide additional help after birth.

This person-to-person compassion is so different from what San Francisco normally has offered: $320 to $390 per month to its thousands of single, homeless residents, plus food, shelter, clothes, and medicine. That stipend, supplemented by panhandling, enabled the homeless to stay in misery and—according to National Public Radio—"preserve the city's reputation for compassion." San

Francisco compassion, according to the *Christian Science Monitor* on March 5, 2002, means that "urinating in public is a cherished right," as is dying on the streets from drug overdose. The *Monitor* portrayed one San Franciscan "looking at a panhandler wrapped in a tattered and filthy blanket" and saying, "This guy here, you can't get him to follow somebody else's rules."

Mrs. McIlhenny noted that in San Francisco the "cost of living is one of the highest in the nation, jobs are few, and the city is crowded, making it a hotbed for homelessness and crime." But is that an excuse for homeless individuals not to have to follow anyone's rules? "It's not tough to be homeless in San Francisco," the *San Diego Union* quoted one of the Bay Area's homeless men as saying. It is tough for those who are mentally ill; they deserve help, but those who disable themselves don't need a road to further destruction paved with a few dollars. They need encouragement to once again see themselves as made in God's image, no matter how many layers of caked-over dirt are in the way. Some Christians now are offering that encouragement, for—as Mrs. McIlhenny notes, "In San Francisco, an evangelical Christian is either made to put up or shut up!" Other citizens may be catching on: In November 2002, San Franciscans voted to eliminate most direct cash payments to homeless individuals and emphasize individual help instead.

The worst city according to the *Money* magazine list, #328 Miami, is now the poorest U.S. city with a population of at least 250,000. One of every three Miami children is raised in poverty. Over half of Miami-Dade County's 2.25 million residents are foreign born. While those fleeing Cuba a generation ago often brought professional and entrepreneurial skills with them, every hurricane, earthquake, and economic or political crisis now brings more unskilled people from the Caribbean basin and other points south, to what the *Miami Herald* calls "the capital of Latin America." In 2002 state government could not prime the pump, wisely or unwisely, because agencies in Tallahassee faced budget shortfalls. Local government was known largely for political corruption and battles for control between blacks and Latinos. Partly out of desperation, officials pleaded for help from religious groups.

That's where the Family & Children Faith Coalition (FCFC), a gathering of 300 Miami churches and faith-based ministries, made a difference in 2002 by bringing groups together through the establishment of faith-based Neighborhood Resource Centers. One such center, in the Little Havana section of Miami (now home for new immigrants from Nicaragua, El Salvador, Argentina, and other countries), houses English language classes, employment and food services, a preschool, and other programs that include presentations about Christ and attempts to connect newcomers with local churches. FCFC's main job is to train leaders, gather demographics, and find funding and potential partners.

Part of the training comes at monthly gatherings focused on specific issues such as youth mentoring, addiction recovery, foster care, or domestic violence. FCFC also set up jobs partnerships between businesses and religious groups and works to increase the reach of Christian daycare centers, the number of foster/adopting parents in churches, and the access of poor children to medical care.

"LOOK HOW THEY LOVE ONE ANOTHER"

With such social entrepreneurial work going on in virtually all of the cities on the *Money* magazine list, a few journalists ask why. A few are like Pachomius, a pagan Roman soldier around A.D. 400, who saw Christians bringing food to those falling before famine and disease. As Alvin Schmidt writes in *Under the Influence: How Christianity Transformed Civilization*, Pachomius "learned that they were people of a special religion and were called Christians. Curious to understand a doctrine which inspired them with so much humanity, he studied it, and that was the beginning of his conversion."

Pachomius's education shows us that the current manifestations of Christian compassion are part of an old tradition that challenged even an older one. Plato argued that an ill slave or poor man unable to work should be left to die. Two centuries before Christ, Plautus told his fellow Romans, "You do a beggar bad service by giving him food and drink; you lose what you give and prolong his life for more misery." But Christianity stood out in the eyes of Pachomius because it was so different from the exchange religions of his era (and ours). In an exchange religion, a person gives to a god (libations, obeisance, corpses of enemies), and the god will reciprocate. The social customs of ancient Rome were applied theology. Romans practicing *liberalitas* would give to those more wealthy or powerful, thus maximizing the return on their investments.

Christians who understood grace—God helping those who were poor in spirit—were different. They applied their theology through the practice of *caritas*, which meant helping the economically poor without expecting anything in return. The voluntary nature of Christian charity also grew out of the biblical sense of God, who blesses and withholds blessing on His own volition. Rome's Emperor Trajan near the end of the first century A.D. banned voluntary associations of Christians, thinking they were not good for the health of the state—and he was right, because when Christians helped the poor, the state had less opportunity to step in and aggrandize itself.

The theologian Tertullian a century later defended Christian voluntary associations, saying they spend their money not on heavy drinking and feasting but on helping the poor, orphans, and old people. He added, "It is our care for the helpless, our practice of lovingkindness that brands us in the eyes of many of our opponents. 'Only look,' they say, 'how they love one another.'"

Occasionally that love today breaks through barriers. Churches that develop social welfare programs can win respect. The *Los Angeles Times* has shown hostility toward biblical Christians in recent decades, but the newspaper's Sunday magazine on July 21, 2002, favorably portrayed Matthew Barnett, pastor of the city's "Dream Center," an inner-city church with 200 ministries emerging from it.

The ministries include a Christian school, a vocational training center, a medical center, a neighborhood redevelopment center, a recording studio, a Skid Row outreach program, and programs for various minorities.

Many journalists still have problems understanding that the impulse toward obedience to God that creates what they like also creates what they don't like. Evidence of Christians loving one another, and non-Christians as well, is readily available, if more journalists would stop mailing in formula stories about nasty evangelicals and start seeing the diversity of Christian activity. I don't want to suggest that journalists covering Christian compassion should abandon criticism; in fact, some knowledge of American history leads to a far deeper critique of the Protestant role than comes out in the easy, drive-by cultural shootings.

Here's an example of conventional journalistic wisdom. Bill Mittlefehldt of the *St. Paul Pioneer Press* wrote in June, 2002, that "Religious hatred and intolerance inspired the al-Qaida terrorist attacks. Our nation's founders knew that a young nation, filled with immigrants of different nationalities, languages and religions, could easily pull apart. This is why public schools were designed as nonsectarian institutions—to unite 'we the people.'"

That's not accurate. Public (that is, government-funded, nonchurch) schooling caught on in the 1840s and thereafter, after the nation's founders were gone. Many schools were not so much nonsectarian as antisectarian, and anti one faith in particular, Catholicism. Catholics, perceiving the public schools as devoted to teaching Protestantism, worked to set up their own institutions and asked that some of their tax money be used to defray expenses. The response was ugly: Opposition among Protestants to the growing number of Catholic immigrants, largely from Ireland, and concern that children going to Catholic schools would grow up to oppose American liberty led to riots in the 1840s and 1850s. One Philadelphia riot in 1844 resulted in thirteen deaths and the burning down of a Catholic church.

Some writers wanted to stop all immigration, but others looked to public schools to save America. An article in *The Massachusetts Teacher* in 1851 stated that children of immigrants "must be taught as our own children are taught. We say *must be*, because in many cases this can only be accomplished by coercion. . . . The children must be gathered up and forced into school, and those who resist or impede this plan, whether parents or *priests*, must be held accountable and punished." The Wisconsin Teachers' Association declared in 1865 that "children are the property of the state."

Ironically, the public schools weren't doing much to teach Protestantism. The intellectual leader of the public school movement was Horace Mann, a Unitarian who pushed for largely secularized public schools and overcame opposition from Protestants by assuring them that daily readings from the King James Bible and generic moral instruction could continue. He succeeded largely because of bigotry and over the objections of theologians such as R. L. Dabney (the Stonewall Jackson aide), who explained that teaching a person how to use a saw could be done in a value-neutral way, but "dexterity in an art is not education. The latter nurtures a soul, the other only drills a sense-organ or muscle; the one has a mechanical end, the other a moral."

Nevertheless, bigotry was so rampant that some Protestants were content to try teaching in a religion-less way as long as Catholics would be hard-pressed to maintain their own school system. President Ulysses S. Grant, who called Catholicism a center of "superstition, ambition and ignorance," proposed in 1875 a Constitutional amendment that would require states to establish government-funded schools, forbid those schools to teach any religious tenets, and prohibit any government funds from going to religious schools. James Blaine, the Republican leader in the House of Representatives, introduced the amendment the following week, and it became known as the Blaine Amendment.

The amendment was instantly controversial. Vermont Senator

Justin Morrill wrote, "The Catholics will rave, but I suppose there is not one who ever voted for free-men, free-schools, or the Republican party in war or peace." It easily passed the House of Representatives but was defeated in the Senate, and Blaine lost out in his attempt to become president in 1884. Nevertheless, thirty-seven states during the late 1800s and early 1900s inserted into their state constitutions versions of the Blaine Amendment, sometimes under duress. Congress often required Western territories seeking admission to the Union to have the amendments in their state constitutions. Ironically but biblically (the book of Proverbs notes that "he who digs a pit falls into it"), those amendments are now a major barrier to school choice across the country and to any government funds going to Christian schools.

Arizona's supreme court recently called that state's Blaine Amendment "a clear manifestation of . . . bigotry" and did not let it sideline a tax credit law that furthers school choice. In 2000 Justice Clarence Thomas attacked the Blaine Amendments by name, noting, "Hostility to aid to pervasively sectarian schools has a shameful pedigree that we do not hesitate to disavow." He emphasized that "this doctrine, born of bigotry, should be buried now." If journalists had covered this story, they would have been able to attack accurately the evangelical arrogance of the past, find out today who is willing to have a level playing field for all religions, and see who is pushing for supremacy for his particular worldview.

FUNERALS IMAGINED AND REAL

Many journalists still look upon Christianity as a cold blast from the past. Thomas Jefferson predicted two centuries ago that belief in the Bible as divinely inspired would die out in America. Clarence Darrow predicted the same thing in the 1920s following his rhetorical victory in the Scopes trial. In 1980 the mayor of Los Angeles favored banning Bible studies in private homes.

Journalists have tended to act toward Christianity as an old woman acted toward her husband who lay dying in his bed. He suddenly smelled the aroma of his favorite chocolate chip cookies wafting up the stairs. He gathered his remaining strength. With great effort he forced himself down the stairs and gazed into the kitchen. Spread out upon platters on the kitchen table were hundreds of cookies. Mustering one great final effort, he threw himself toward the table. His aged and withered hand shakily made its way to a cookie at the edge of the table—but then his wife suddenly smacked it with a spatula. "Stay out of those," she roared. "They're for the funeral."

Despite the predictions of Jefferson, Darrow, and others, Christianity's funeral has not come. That's because those who stand on the rock of Christ, whether they are famous athletes such as Warner and Smoltz or little-known warriors such as those who choose to live in the inner cities of Memphis or Miami, find that solid ground exists nowhere else. While Christianity has survived, ideologies such as communism and fascism have withered, and intellectual constructs such as existentialism have witnessed attempts at subjective solidity breaking into nothingness.

Christians need to communicate to journalists that in good times it's easy to put aside questions of meaning, but when faced with illness or imprisonment, all of us see that sinking sand offers inadequate support. Two decades ago Armando Valladares, a Cuban Christian who objected to the direction of Fidel Castro's revolution and was imprisoned for twenty-two years, testified before the U.N. Commission on Human Rights on what happens without the hope supplied by Christ. He spoke of how one night "a political prisoner named Fernando Lopez del Toro came to my cell. In a tone of despair, he said to me that what hurt the most, out of all of the torment, was that our sacrifice might be in vain. It was not the pain, but the apparent uselessness of enduring it that was defeating Fernando."

Valladares described how "Fernando climbed up on his bunk, coiled a dirty towel around his neck, and with a sharp piece of metal tore open his skin, searched with his fingers for the jugular vein, and in one stroke cut it. He died a few minutes later. Fernando was the victim of indifference, of silence, of that terrible echoless universe in which, in this century of horrors and violations, so many good men and women die." Valladares's plea is one that many Christians have taken to heart, and many secular journalists should as well:

> We must raise our voices without fear and use all available means in defense of those who are persecuted. We have to shout about the pain that they suffer and we must accuse their executioners without fear. We have to reach into the cells of all the world's Fernando Lopez del Toros to tell them with firmness and solidarity, "Listen, do not take your life; men of good will are with you. In some corner, in your honor and in your memory, there will always be the note of a violin, the voice of compassion of those who will defend you. Look, you are not an animal. Do not take your life. Liberty will never disappear from the face of the earth."

In the American liberty theme park, we need to remember how to defend true liberty against those who oppose it or abuse it. Come what may, Christians should never fall into the despair of Fernando Lopez del Toro, because even in prison the conclusion of the hymn "For All the Saints" should resound in our ears:

> *And when the fight is fierce, the warfare long,*
> *Steals on the ear the distant triumph song,*
> *And hearts are brave again, and arms are strong,*
> > *Alleluia!*

> *From earth's wide bounds, from ocean's farthest coast,*
> *Through gates of pearl streams in the countless host,*
> *Singing to Father, Son, and Holy Ghost,*
> > *Alleluia!*

4

DEFINING THE
INTERNATIONAL STAKES

Christians should continue to point out sin calmly and compassionately, but instead of emphasizing complaints, we should demonstrate commitment both domestically and internationally. Dayna Curry and Heather Mercer, the two missionaries freed late in 2001 from Taliban captivity, did just that in Afghanistan, and they received respectful but puzzled coverage. For example, the June 30, 2002, *Austin American-Statesman* described the "two grateful and gracious women" affectionately but was irate about their plans to return to Afghanistan: "How dare these Americans endanger their own lives—and those of innocents—by tempting fate yet again, carrying Christianity to cultures that forbid it?"

The article concluded, "In the end, there is no understanding Curry and Mercer without accepting the unsettling incongruence that seems to define them." The incongruence? When the two young women change soiled hospital bedding, their "commitment to charity seems to transcend any type of faith-based agenda," but they are guilty of "showing a Jesus video, reading Christian stories to children, inviting Christian dialogue with Muslim citizens." Secular liberals are unsettled by the thought that offering material help in the hospital might go along with offering spiritual help to neighbors. Relief and evangelism as two sides of the same coin? Too expensive a proposition for a secularist.

Many mainstream reporters have trouble understanding that Christians are Christians not because we conform to a certain set of propositions or rules, but because we accept God's sovereignty over our lives. That means we are to follow what the Bible says even when it seems incongruous to current managers of the liberty theme park. For example, European reporters who interviewed me during 1999 and 2000, when I was an informal advisor to the Bush campaign, had a hard time seeing how I could be pro-life and also favor (in principle) the death penalty for murder. One wrote, "The issue that seems contradictory to me is that the same people who are pro-life for babies seem to be pro-death for adults."

For a person to be both pro-life and pro-death would be inconsistent. However, defining the position as pro-innocent-life makes the inconsistency disappear. Abortion is about killing the innocent while the death penalty is about killing the guilty. It's important, of course, that capital punishment be used only on those who have committed murder beyond the shadow of a doubt. It's important to allow full appeals and full checking and rechecking of the court record so that the innocent are preserved and that guilty people of favored races or genders don't escape justice. Overall, it makes sense for a pro-life person to hang tough on capital punishment for those who deliberately take away life, and this can be explained to journalists.

There's more though: More important than whether a position makes sense to us is whether it makes sense to God. The Old Testament prescribed the death penalty for murder not only among the Israelites but in other nations as well. Christ turned the other cheek to personal insults but upheld all the standards of justice laid down by the Father in heaven. As American citizens we pledge to respect the Constitution even though it was written by limited and fallible men (and for that reason we reserve the right to amend it). If we praise the Constitution, how much more should we respect something done not by fallible man but by an infallible God? And since the Bible upholds the principle of capital punishment, shouldn't we also—while remaining open to improving the practice? We need to show journalists that the Bible is our constitution, and we are to act as strict constructionists concerning it. That means, since Christ fed the 5,000 and 4,000 in conjunction with teaching them, we should do the same. We need to offer the needy in Afghanistan and around the world both material and spiritual food. If we redistribute material in the same way that secularists do, we are unfaithful, loose constructionists.

LOOKING FOR LOVE IN ALL THE WRONG PLACES

A little over four decades ago, at a time when the focus of the Cold War was on the then-divided city of Berlin, President John F. Kennedy offered a challenge. He declared, "There are many people in the world who really don't understand, or say they don't, what is the great issue between the Free World and the communist world. Let them come to Berlin. There are some who say that communism is the wave of the future. Let them come to Berlin." That was the hot spot, and a vital one. Marxist propagandists were telling their captive audiences that however unsatisfactory life was within the Soviet empire, the West was decadent. But the Berliners showed that they were tough enough to put up with hardship. And the West stuck with them.

Today, radical Muslims depict the United States as a land ruled by selfishness and fueled by the love of money and perversity. They are partially right in those descriptions because the America of moral anarchy does exist. But these radical Muslims also need to acknowledge the other America, the one of incredible compassion, the one with people willing to sacrifice to provide for widows, orphans, the aged, and the disabled. This other America isn't in the spotlight. It's a land of moms and pops like the Montagues helping sons and daughters with cerebral palsy in small towns and large cities, without publicity agents.

Most journalists I've met do not know that the other America exists; so they cannot tell the world to come to the Berlins of compassion. As we have seen, many journalists approach Christianity out of ignorance and fear (and sometimes, perhaps, malice). They think of Christianity in terms of the bigot they stared at or the televangelist they sneered at. If they have any religious interest at all, they tend to see the grass as greener in the next religion's yard.

One liberal publication, *The New Republic*, acknowledged this attraction in its issue the week before the 9/11 disaster. Joshua Kurlantzick wrote that his view of Buddhism "was shaped by the American media, which usually portrays Buddhists as pure, serene, and incorruptible." But then he attended a Buddhist seminar in Bangkok and spoke with Thais who told him of "saffron-robed Buddhist monks guilty of graft, lechery, and other crimes." Kurlantzick first "chuckled skeptically at their tales," but then he found the stories of rape, orgiastic sex, and murder to be true and "especially shocking because so many Westerners assume Buddhism to be fundamentally different from other faiths. It isn't. . . . Not that any of this is undermining Buddhism's reputation in the West. . . . American disciples won't let reality get in the way of their preconceptions about the religion." They see some other religion as a way of gaining what they view as freedom.

Some journalists are attracted to Buddhism, a faith often portrayed as anti-materialistic. They write about monks going out begging with only two robes, a bowl (for begging, eating, and drinking), and a strainer to remove insects from what they drink (that's for the benefit of the insects). They see the itinerant monk as free. But their superficial portrait is inaccurate even for those who do fit the stereotype because what Buddhist theologians typically advocate is non-attachment, which means not bonding to people or things. The Buddha 2,500 years ago left behind his young wife; today if an advanced Buddhist man is tempted to fall in love with a beautiful woman, he may be told to imagine her as a corpse or to visualize her intestines at work.

The appeal of Buddhism is one example of a technique familiar to vendors of both cars and ideas: bait and switch. In business that means attracting a customer and then switching him or her to a more expensive or similarly-priced-but-inferior product. In theology the process can be similar. Many Americans with poetic sensibilities see Buddhism's anti-materialism as liberating, but they do not understand its non-attachment philosophy. Tennyson's lapidary line, "Better to have loved and lost, than never to have loved at all," has thrilled many romantics, but a Buddhist priest who spoke to my University of Texas class frankly admitted that if Tennyson had been a Buddhist, he would not have written those words. Young people baited by romantic ideas either leave Buddhism or, if they are in it too far, accept the romance-less vision of avoiding attachment to anyone who will one day die—which means everyone.

Many sects within Hinduism also dangle the bait of liberating anti-materialism and then switch devotees to non-attachment. Other parts of standard Hindu theory have serious health consequences that generally go unmentioned in U.S. press reports. Oft-praised rules against killing animals have led to human malnutrition, while insecticide-free fields and poorly defended storage bins provide feasts for insects and rats. Hindus over the centuries have had the liberty to starve. The concept of karma has also hurt health by creating an internal fatalism so that people do not take steps to protect themselves or fight disease. Karma reduces any interest in helping the poor, who are seen as getting exactly what they deserve. Holding up begging as holy has led to disrespect for hard work and constructive competition.

False ideas of liberation also have consequences when carried out in nonreligious pursuits. For example, movies, ads, and talk shows all suggest to men especially that either being single or acting that way offers varieties of physical pleasure and a sense of psychological conquest. Surveys show that the reality is very different, and just what we would expect from reading the Bible: Married sex beats unmarried sex in both quality and quantity. But that's not what some people who view only the lies of both popular and high culture would suspect. A few of those who live the lie throughout their twenties and thirties may somehow skip their way through the minefields of abortion, broken hearts, and disease, but as young bodies become old, alienation and loneliness tend to edge out lust. When reality doesn't sink in until age forty or fifty, lost decades cannot be replaced. The situation is better for people who get married, but then a false understanding of freedom frequently leads to divorce.

Ideologies have also benefited from grass-is-greener yearning coupled with misunderstanding. Ironically, many liberals during the 1930s embraced the greatest enslaving movement of the twentieth century—communism. Some in the 1960s became supporters of Cuba's Castro, China's Mao, or the Soviet Union's Brezhnev, even though their prisons were filled with those who had defended family-based freedom. Communism's bait-and-switch attracted those who did not realize the complications inherent in defining the results of Karl Marx's mantra, "From each according to his ability, to each according to his need." Beyond a bare minimum of calories and shelter, what are needs, as opposed to wants and desires? "Power to the people," but which people? The classic Marxist saying should more accurately have concluded, "To each according to his demand for power—and his viciousness toward those seen as obstacles."

THE NEW FANTASY

Since the 9/11 disaster, the most significant illusions have involved Islam. Leading journalists fought the religious wave that began on the sad day (as chapter 2 pointed out) by arguing that fervently held religion was the enemy. Islam is not the new Marxism. American journalists are not going to Baghdad and saying, as famed muckraker Lincoln Steffens did in 1930 after traveling to Moscow, "I have gone over into the future, and it works." But an analogy to the 1950s might be helpful. Few liberal U.S. journalists were communists during the 1950s, but almost *all* opposed anti-communism. Today liberal journalists are not flocking to Islam, but their standard position is anti-anti-Islam.

Reporters regularly suggest that Christian and Muslim "fundamentalism" are the same and that mainstream Islam is peace-loving and moderate like mainline Protestant denominations. In late September, 2001, the America On Line primer on "Understanding Islam" sported this heading: "Same God: Muslims accept the teachings of the Jewish Torah and the Christian Gospels." At that time the PBS website proclaimed, "One should properly say that Muslims worship God, not Allah, which is simply the word for God (with a capital G) in the Arabic language. Giving a different name to the one God worshiped by the followers of Muhammad erroneously implies that their God is different from the one God worshiped by Jews or Christians."

That's an easy statement to make for the reporter who does not believe in either God or Allah; adherence to one or the other seems like deciding between the Mickey Mouse club and the Donald Duck club. But it takes neither a rocket scientist nor a theological genius to see essential differences between Christianity and Islam—and a refusal to depict Islam accurately will leave the United States unable to deal realistically with the greatest external danger we now face. Here are ten differences between Islam and Christianity, along with their implications.

1. The God of the Bible sees humans as sinners and is grieved by our disobedience. God is portrayed as a husband who feels pain because of an unfaithful wife or as a father brokenhearted by his children's rebellion. Allah, on the other hand, sends prophets who warn people, but if those people disobey, so be it. The Noah stories of the Quran and the Bible provide a good basis for comparison. In Sura 71 of the Quran, Noah warns his people, they disobey, they drown in the flood. Game, set, match. Same thing happens in the Bible, but there God's "heart was filled with pain" (Genesis 6:6).

The Bible states that God adopts us into His family. The Quran emphasizes that a just master allows us to be his servants, but not his children. Biblical passages about God's majesty have their parallels in the Quran. But look at the biblical passages that emphasize God's tenderness, showing Him as a father teaching His child to walk or as a shepherd carrying a lamb in His arms (Deuteronomy 1:31; Hosea 11:1-4; Isaiah 40:11). Those do not have their parallels in the Quran.

2. The Old Testament (Isaiah 53:5 NIV) describes the Messiah as one who "was pierced for our transgressions, he was crushed for our iniquities; the punishment that brought us peace was upon him, and by his wounds we are healed." The New Testament, in Hebrews 4:15-16 NIV, makes the significance of this clear: "We do not have a high priest who is unable to sympathize with our weaknesses, but we have one who has been tempted in every way, just as we are—yet was without sin. Let us then approach the throne of grace with confidence, so that we may receive mercy and find grace to help us in our time of need."

Muslims view the rejected and wounded Jesus Christ as one of perhaps 124,000 messengers or prophets Allah has sent, not as the Messiah. But Muslims do not believe Jesus died when crucified. They do not believe He was resurrected. They do not see Him as the permanent high priest who has been through what we've been through and offers grace from a position of intimate understanding.

3. Within Islam that unbiblical depiction makes logical sense. The Quran states that in the Garden of Eden Adam and Eve both erred, then repented and were forgiven, with no consequences from their rebellion: "Adam learnt from his Lord certain words and his Lord forgave him." Allah then made Adam his deputy (caliph) and the first of the prophets. Since Adam and Eve did not sin, and since all of us, their descendants, do not by nature sin—man is basically good but mistake-prone—God need not redeem us. Instead, strong, sinless leaders can arise to lead us.

Christians, realizing that all have sinned and fall short of God's glory, tend to be skeptical. Muslims have a tendency to revere strong leaders who put forth an image of perfection. Christians read in the Bible honest reporting about twisted, sinful individuals whom God chose not because of their own righteousness but because of His love. Muslims, though, see a record of great heroes that Jews and Christians somehow twisted during centuries of transmission.

4. Because Muslims think we can be sinless if we have strong character and follow all the rules, they have lots of rules, and very specific ones. Some of these are terrific, emphasizing humility: Don't boast about how you've contributed to build a mosque. Don't set up elaborate grave markers. Don't wear clothes just designed to attract attention. Some are common sense: Don't defecate near a place where people draw water. Some rules are incredibly precise: Do not eradicate insects by burning them because fire is to be used only on rats, scorpions, crows, kites, and mad dogs. Do not read the Quran in a house where there is a dog unless the dog is used for hunting, farming, or herding livestock.

The nature of Islamic prayer periods during the day is also rule-driven. Each time of prayer is made up of units containing set sequences of standing, bowing, kneeling, and prostrating while reciting verses from the Quran or other prayer formulas. The sequences are repeated twice at dawn prayer, three times at sunset prayer, and four times at noon, afternoon, and evening prayers. No deviation is allowed. Muslims do not gain a sense of liberty from their religion.

5. Christianity by its very nature is about the one and the many, monotheism with a trinity. Muslims think there is a tension in holding firmly to both, and they are right. That tension has pushed Christians to build a society that emphasizes both unity and diversity and in that way reflects the Trinity. That tension also allows for the development of a liberty theme park.

Muslims often find diversity suspicious. For example, they are suspicious of the many different authors who produced the Bible over a period of more than 1,000 years. They look amiss at the story of Christ's life and death given in four separate Gospels: If there are four separate accounts, they must all be false. The Quran, seen as having come through one mediator over twenty-three years, is much more credible.

6. The emphasis on *tawhid*—making everything united—has huge cultural implications. In the book of Genesis, Abraham questioned God about the destruction of Sodom, but the word *islam* means "submission." This carries over into a reluctance to accept the legitimacy of critics. Salman Rushdie had to hide to preserve his life, and a host of other critics of Islam have been knifed or shot. Concerning intellectual liberty in Muslim countries, Hisham Kassem of the Egyptian Organization for Human Rights said, "It's not safe to think in this part of the world."

Although the Quran declares that "there is no compulsion in religion," Islamic states often interpret that to mean that "there is no competition in religion" within their borders. Iraq, Iran, Syria, Saudi Arabia, Sudan, Pakistan, Indonesia, Kuwait, and Egypt are some of the countries blasted in the State Department's year 2000 *Report on International Religious Freedom*. In hard-core Muslim countries, any Muslim who violates *tawhid* by becoming a Christian may forfeit his life, family, or property. In several "moderate" Muslim countries, churches are allowed behind walls within which Bibles and church bulletins must remain.

7. The emphasis on unicity also has governmental implications. Without a sense of original sin, Lord Acton's concern about the corrupting potential of centralized power does not arise. A system of checks and balances seems redundant, and dictators abound. Originally, Islamic countries had no separation between religious and civil law, between Islam and the state, and that is the way radical Muslims want things to be once again. According to this thinking, Islamic societies should not shape laws to fit their specific histories; they are to submit.

Because Islam in many ways trains people not to govern themselves but to be governed by dictates, Muslim countries almost always are run by dictators. Those rulers have had much in common with the rulers of Marxist countries. It's not surprising that Egypt, Syria, Iraq, Libya, and other countries in the 1960s turned away from the United States even though the United States successfully pressured British, French, and Israeli forces to withdraw from the Suez Canal in 1956. It's not surprising now that terrorists from Marxist remnants and radical Islam work well together.

8. The father-son relationship that exists between God and redeemed man in Christianity, as opposed to the master-slave relationship of Islam, also has its tensions. Fathers face conflicting impulses: Do you hug a child with a mild injury, or do you tell him to be a man? That leads to a creative tension between soft and hard in Christianity, a tension that comes out in the compassionate conservative goal of being tough-minded but tenderhearted, a tension between God's holiness and God's mercy that is resolved through Christ's sacrifice.

That tension does not exist in Islam with its master-slave relationship. Nor does Islam understand compassion—suffering with the poor in the way that Christianity does. Jesus tasted hostility from men and knew what it was to be unjustly tortured and abandoned, to endure overwhelming loss, and eventually be killed. Muhammad encountered opposition but died in his bed with his wives ministering to him.

9. In Christianity the church is the bride of Christ, who gave His life for her; husbands are to love their wives enough to die for them. The husband-wife relationship in Islam also mirrors its theology, which means marriage is in many ways a master-slave relationship. Men can beat their wives, although Muslim apologists say only a light tap is socially correct. Men get four wives and keep the kids if they divorce one; Muslim apologists defend polygamy by pointing to American adultery and trophy wives, but our cultural embarrassments do not justify institutionalized humiliation. Genital mutilation, although not in the Quran, is practiced on one in five Muslim girls.

Different understandings lead to very different laws. Here's one of the well-known strict laws: Cut off at the wrist the right hand of a thief even if he makes restitution and pledges never to steal again. That's very different from the Bible, which has a thief paying back what he has stolen and asking for forgiveness. (What has to be paid back depends on what he stole, whether he has already disposed of the item, and whether he shows repentance. Amounts given in the Bible include two, four, or five times what he stole, but never is he maimed for life.)

10. Christianity, in short, is the religion of the second chance. With Islam it's often one strike and you're out. Jesus tells the woman caught in adultery, after he has shamed those condemning her, "Go and sin no more." One Hadith tells about a woman pregnant by adultery coming to Muhammad. He has her treated decently until she gives birth and then has her stoned to death. Islam teaches that Allah loves the righteous, but Christianity teaches that "While we were still sinners, Christ died for us" (Rom. 5:8).

In a religion of grace we don't have to be worried about being zapped at any moment when we deviate from the rules. Muslims, though, try to sleep, eat, drink, and even dress as Muhammad did. They try to repeat the special prayers he uttered upon going to sleep and waking up, or even upon entering and leaving the bathroom. Islamic scholars have developed an enormous list of what to do and what not to do—and that raises the question of what happens to those who break some of the rules.

WHAT, THEN, DO WE DO ALL DAY?

Do the two religions lead adherents to act in similar ways? Muslim and Christian "fundamentalists" differ greatly in how they relate religion and politics. Islam has no division between church and state. In Islam mosque dominates state, and the state decrees that the mosque cannot have competition. In Muslim countries churches cannot be built within half a mile of a mosque, and only the head of state can allow new churches to be built or old ones restored. Muslim Brotherhood leader Hasan al-Banna noted that in Islam "politics is part of religion . . . for its teaching is not, 'Give to Caesar what is Caesar's and to God what is God's,' but rather, 'Caesar and what is Caesar's are to the one and only victorious God.'"

Even the Muslim calendar dates not from Muhammad's first revelation in A.D. 610, but from when he became a political leader during his Mecca-to-Medina journey in 622. Muhammad is the only founder of a major religion to have headed a government; Jesus and Buddha certainly did not. Muslims, without a belief in original sin, advocate placing unified power in the hands of those considered virtuous.

Journalists since 9/11 have also emphasized high points of Islamic history such as the civilization that made great advances in science, medicine, and mathematics, and Islam's success in gaining probably over one billion adherents—only 15 percent of them Arabs—by welcoming people of every skin color and ethnicity. The high points are well worth reporting, but journalists should not be ignoring low points such as the Arab development of the slave trade.

Journalistic unwillingness to write anything negative about Islam may be due to self-protection, but journalists are supposed to be like firefighters: When others are running out of buildings, reporters are to run in. Journalistic unwillingness may also be due to the desire to be peacemakers, but only telling the truth can lead to long-range peace. Journalists should not shy away from quoting bloody Quran verses such as Sura 8:39: "And fight with them until there is no more persecution and religion should be only for Allah." Or 9:14: "Fight them, Allah will punish them by your hands and bring them to disgrace." Or 9:29: "Fight those who do not believe in Allah . . . until they pay the tax in acknowledgment of superiority and they are in a state of subjection."

Islamic scholars in turn point to exterminate-the-Canaanite passages in the book of Joshua, to which Jews and Christians reply that those writings reflect special circumstances, to which Muslims say,

"So do ours." Thrusts and parries can continue on those lines, but it's clear that Jesus was a man of peace, Muhammad at times a man of war. Christians read the Old Testament's bloody passages in the light of the New. Muslims have nothing to take the edge off their violent passages. Christianity initially spread through non-aggressive means, especially the blood of martyrs, while Islam initially spread in large part through military conflict, with the blood of its opponents often flowing.

Furthermore, Christianity held up its peaceful dead for imitation, Islam its warlike victors. No Bible verses promise salvation to those who die in war, but many Quranic verses promise that good things will happen to all who die in a campaign to spread Islam. "Those who fly in Allah's way and are then slain or die," Sura 22:58 promises, "Allah will most certainly grant them a goodly sustenance, and most surely Allah is the best Giver of sustenance." Some of Muhammad's sayings promise that those who die fighting for Allah will receive special benefits.

GUILT AND NEGLIGENCE

The reluctance of some reporters to note these differences may also stem from Western guilt. It became fashionable during the Clinton years to apologize to the Muslim world for a variety of American offenses. Secretary of State Madeleine Albright apologized for U.S. support of Iran's shah and the U.S. favoring of Iraq during the Iran-Iraq War. Bill Clinton took it upon himself in 1999 to apologize to Iran and the Middle East for having suffered "a lot of abuse from various Western nations. . . . You have a right to be angry at something my country or my culture or others that are generally allied with us today did to you 50 or 60 or 100 or 150 years ago." Two months after 9/11, Bill Clinton was still talking about atrocities that occurred during the Crusades and implying, since "terror has a long history," that we should not retaliate thoroughly for the death of 3,000 persons on September 11, 2001.

Once the initial fury following 9/11 diminished, many journalists tried to reduce concern by giving only half-truths. It's true that mainstream Islam never considered "self-martyrdom" a guarantee of immediate access to Paradise. Muslims over the centuries have condemned arson and attacks on travelers or other innocent victims, whether Muslim or non-Muslim. Even if another country's attacks have created civilian casualties among Muslims, traditional Islam still does not justify terrorist acts, because the injustice of others does not create a license to kill. Nor are historical grievances concerning the Crusades supposed to justify brutal revenge nine centuries later.

The problem, though, is that while Muslims agree that it's not right to attack civilians or innocent bystanders, some are making up new definitions of noncombatant categories. Some Palestinian groups war on every Israeli, conveniently claiming that almost all Israeli citizens receive some military training; so few are civilians and no one is innocent. It's only one step from that to claim that every Pentagon worker is an enemy because the U.S. supports Israel. It's one step further to declare everyone at the World Trade Center an enemy because capitalists control the world. It's a further step beyond to state, as bin Laden did in 1999 to *Newsweek*, that "any American who pays taxes to his government . . . is our target, because he is helping the American war machine against the Muslim nation."

Journalists have not written much about how, at various times in Muslim history, factions arose that took extra steps down what can quickly become a slippery slope. The Kharajites became infamous within early Islam for murdering Muslims who disagreed with them. Centuries later some Muslims who used hashish to get themselves ready to kill originated the word *assassin*. Orthodox Muslims saw these killers as evil and viewed them much the way Christians today see Ku Klux Klan clowns who claim to be Christian but live lives of hatred. But, with Islam's early history of violence and its tendency to respect dictators pushing for unicity, violent movements within Islam continued to rise and received substantial support.

U.S. newspapers during the first year after 9/11 rarely spelled out the connection between the Saudi Arabian government and the Sunni Islamic sect known as Wahhabism from which bin Laden's terrorists generally came. Founded by Ibn Abdul Wahhab (1703-1792), Wahhabis from the start were willing to kill civilians who opposed them. They did just that in the city of Qarbala in 1801, leaving 2,000 people dead. In the nineteenth and early twentieth centuries, Wahhabis opposed the decadence of the Ottoman Turk empire. Now they are out to overthrow "the American empire" and have trained a generation of students for that pursuit through a network of madrassahs (religious boarding schools) funded by Saudi oil money.

The combination of anti-anti-communism and anti-anti-Islamism leave journalists reluctant to point out how the Wahhabi wing of Islam and the "national liberation" wing of Marxism had made common cause by attacking a free enterprise system in which people prosper by fulfilling the needs and desires of others. That some of those desires lack virtue is all the excuse Wahhabis need to join the neo-Marxist assault on capitalism. And like many U.S. professors in the late 1960s who followed students instead of leading them, some Islamic clerics who know better have bowed to the extremists. The head of Egypt's Al-Azhar University, the Harvard of the Muslim world, pleased his students when he agreed (contrary to the Islamic tradition) that self-martyrdom was acceptable.

Other purportedly mainstream Muslims have not spoken out forcefully against terrorists who claim Quranic warrant. Part of the answer is theological, as clerical apologists for terrorism have pointed to particular verses that they say have been ignored or misinterpreted by traditional Islam. But a large part has been simple momentum. Islam has been on an international losing streak during the past several centuries. Many mainstream Muslims, while opposing terrorists theologically, have been unwilling to stand up to those who appeared to be on a winning streak. That's why David Forte of the Hudson Institute has said, "If we have respect for ourselves, if we have respect for Islam, we can no longer tolerate the evil they [the terrorists] represent. Two civilizations hang in the balance." Islam needs reformation, and it needs America to show that Wahhabi Marxism is not the vanguard of the future.

When journalists offer the bait that Allah and God, Islam and Christianity, are really the same, we can feel that peace is at hand. And yet—in another version of what President Bush (in dealing with racism) called "the soft bigotry of low expectations"—we are ignoring the need of Islam to change, and potentially condemning Muslims and us to future war. Many reporters may not care about Muslim reality. As essayist Susan Sontag observed, it has been fashionable to be pro-Islam, and fashion regularly trumps fact.

GOOD NEIGHBORS—BUT GOOD RULERS?

None of this discussion should leave Christians or anyone else unwilling to welcome the presence and contributions of Muslims in America. Several million Muslims now live in the United States. Most have enriched this country and themselves with their work and talents. In our liberty theme park, Muslims are free to worship, and that's as it should be. Members of one mosque—a neat yellow brick building with a green-roofed tower and a minaret—that I visited in the Detroit area were using their freedom to have regular services, lectures, and prayer times. They also put on a Detroit Islam television program and a weekly "Islam Night" complete with Islamic Jeopardy contests, basketball, discussions, and group prayer. They have used their freedom to build a school, the Muslim American Youth Academy, with a cafeteria, gymnasium, computer lab, and lots of classroom space.

Muslims in the United States have also been able to use their economic clout. When a Burger King radio ad had a character with the Islamic name Rasheed reading a poem praising a bacon-cheddar Whopper sandwich, Muslims (observant ones don't eat pork) protested. Burger King officials withdrew the commercial and said they would rewrite it to delete objectionable references. When

Muslims complained about a college textbook, *Marriage and the Family*, that included critical statements about the role of women within Islam, the publisher agreed to delete the offending passages. When a professor at a community college near Detroit did not allow a Muslim student to begin a class presentation with prayer, several hundred Muslims protested, and community college officials rightly apologized.

Muslim-Americans have also received favorable treatment from government bodies in recent years. The Illinois Equal Employment Opportunity Commission ordered that Mohammad Abdullah receive $49,000 from his past employer when he was fired for leaving his job at noon on Fridays for prayer; he regularly arrived early or stayed late to make up the lost time. Fareed Ansari received $105,216 from Ray's Plumbing Contractors in a similar case in Jacksonville, Florida. That's all fine: Employers should try hard to accommodate Muslim believers, and Christian and Jewish believers as well.

What hasn't been fine over the years worldwide has been the treatment of non-Muslims when Muslims grab governmental power. Here's another significant Muslim-Christian difference. When John Ashcroft spoke at Bob Jones University in 1999, he said, "We knew that we were endowed not by the king, but by the Creator, with certain inalienable rights. If America is to be great in the future, it will be if we understand that our source is not civic and temporal, but our source is godly and eternal: Endowed by the Creator with rights of life, liberty and the pursuit of happiness." But as pioneering historian Bat Ye'or has pointed out in *The Dhimmi* and other remarkable books over the past two decades, Islam has no belief in "inalienable rights." Instead, Islam establishes rights for Muslims but gives Jews and Christians living in Muslim-ruled lands a special status as *dhimmis* (Arabic for "protected people").

That word *dhimmi* became historically significant in A.D. 628 when Muhammad's forces defeated a Jewish tribe that lived at the oasis of Khaybar and made with them a treaty known as the *dhimma*. The treaty allowed Jews to continue cultivating their oasis, as long as they gave Muhammad half of their produce. Crucially, Muhammad reserved the right to break the deal and expel the Jews whenever he wished. That agreement has served as a model for Muslims over the centuries.

SECOND-CLASS CITIZENS

Dhimmis—non-Muslims in Muslim lands—typically had to pay discriminatory taxes that cemented their status as second-class citizens. They were on the hook for additional sums payable on Islamic demand. They had to supply forced labor on demand. They were ineligible for any public office and without right even to testify in legal battles. They were not allowed to construct new places of worship, but sometimes they received permission to worship in buildings that predated Muslim conquest. (The buildings had to be dilapidated, with no crosses or bell-ringing allowed, and Muslims were able to ransack them at will.)

Dhimmis were not allowed to possess weapons, marry Muslim women, meet with others on the streets, or ride horses or camels (the two "noble animals"). Dhimmis had to wear special clothes, walk with eyes lowered, and accept being pushed aside by Muslims. Dhimmis had to have low doors on their houses and no lights on the doors. Some particular aspects varied from age to age and region to region. In the ninth century, Jews in some Muslim areas had to wear a patch of white cloth on their shoulders that bore the image of an ape; Christians, since they ate pork, wore a pig image. In the eleventh century Seville Jews could not be met with the greeting, "Peace be unto you," because they were not supposed to have any peace.

The Muslim goal in collecting taxes from dhimmis was to maximize both revenue and abuse. North African nineteenth-century theologian al-Maghali advised that dhimmis be assembled on tax day "in the lowest and dirtiest place," with threatening officials placed above the dhimmis "so that it seems to them, as well as to the others, that our object is to degrade them." With the stage set, al-Maghali advised, officials could play out a little drama of dragging dhimmis "one by one [to the official responsible] for the exacting of payment." They would knock him around and then thrust him aside, making sure he realized that his position would never improve. As al-Maghali put it, "This is the way that the friends of the Lord, of the first and last generations will act toward their infidel enemies, for might belongs to Allah, to His Prophet, and to the Believers."

Other edicts affected not just finances but self-respect. A Cairo rule in 1761 was that "no Jew or Christian may appear on horseback. They ride only asses, and must alight upon meeting even the most lowly Egyptian lord. . . . If the infidel fails to give instant obedience, he is beaten." In Persia in 1890, Jewish women had to "expose their faces in public [like prostitutes]. . . . The men must not wear fine clothes, the only material permitted them being a blue cotton fabric. They are forbidden to wear matching shoes. Every Jew is obliged to wear a piece of red cloth on his chest. A Jew must never overtake a Muslim on a public street. . . . If a Muslim insults a Jew, the latter must drop his head and remain silent. . . . The Jew cannot put on his coat; he must be satisfied to carry it rolled under his arm. . . . It is forbidden for Jews to leave the town or enjoy the fresh air of the countryside. . . . Jews must not consume good fruit."

Muslims showed great patience in psychologically weakening their opponents. For example, authorities would allow bells inside churches but not outside, anticipating that the bells inside would "eventually fall into disuse. For the bells are normally attached to the church steeple so that when rung they may be heard from afar. If they are obliged to ring them within the church, then no one will hear them or pay heed to them and they will be abolished altogether since they will serve no purpose." The result of beatings and belittlements was obvious to observers in Turkey two centuries ago who noted that dhimmis have "the most submissive cringing tone," and in Morocco during the 1870s where it was said Jews had terrorized expressions.

Should that be surprising? Didn't Jews have terrorized expressions in Christian-ruled territories? Bat Ye'or argues that "dhimmi-tude is in no way comparable with the position of Jews in Christendom." Jews in Europe were an oppressed minority. Christians and Jews in many Muslim countries were oppressed majorities. Persecution of a majority is no different ethically than per-secution of a minority, but it requires establishment of a police state rather than just use of the police. "The realm of dhimmitude," Bat Ye'or writes, "is actually situated in a political ideology of permanent war which ruined entire regions, justified massacres, slavery, usurpa-tion of land, and deportations."

DHIMMITUDE VERSUS SERVITUDE

Jacques Ellul, in an introduction to Bat Ye'or's *The Dhimmi*, also dif-ferentiates the situation of the dhimmi from the European serf in the Middle Ages. Serfdom, he notes, "was the result of certain historical changes such as the transformation of slavery . . . when these histor-ical conditions altered, the situation of the serf also evolved until his status finally disappeared." Dhimmi status, though, "was not the product of historical accident but . . . the expression of an absolute, unchanging, theologically grounded Muslim conception of the rela-tionship between Islam and non-Islam. It is not a historical accident of retrospective interest, but a necessary condition of existence."

What are the necessary conditions of existence within an Islamic worldview? Muslims, like Christians, divide people into believers and nonbelievers, but the Islamic conception of future relations between the two is very different. Christians believe that final Christian victory will come not primarily through the efforts of Christians, but only when Christ returns. For Muslims, though, the world is divided into the *dar al-Harb*, land controlled by non-Muslims that forms the "territory of war," and the *dar al-Islam*, the land where Islamic law prevails. This is a permanent state of war, although there may be truces, because it is man's might that will make Islam supreme throughout the world.

In Islam, therefore, a peace is not a peace, and a truce should not last longer than ten years. A time of peace longer than a decade is occasion not for relaxation but for feeling inadequate and fidgety. Infidels should never be allowed to rest on their laurels, famed fourteenth-century Muslim jurist Ibn Taymiyya asserted, because any land they possess is held illegitimately. This means that jihad is not aggression but retrieving what is Islam's legitimate possession. The *dar al-Harb* has no right to exist.

Muslims have long understood the difference between the Islamic and Christian agendas and the way that Muslim centralism can contribute to a mission of permanent war. Ibn Khaldun, who died in 1406, wrote, "In the Muslim community the holy war is a religious duty, because of the universalism of the [Muslim] mission and the obligation to convert everyone to Islam either by persuasion or by force. Therefore, caliphate and royal authority are united [in Islam], so that the person in charge can devote the available strength to both of them [religion and politics] at the same time. The other religious groups did not have a universal mission, and the holy war was not a religious duty to them, save only for purposes of defense."

If Bat Ye'or and Jacques Ellul are right, we should speak about the Muslim assignment of second-class citizenship status not in past tense but in present and future tenses as well. As Ellul writes, "because of Islam's fixed ideological mode. . . . one must know as exactly as possible what the Muslims did with these unconverted conquered peoples, because that is what they will do in the future (and are doing right now)." Based on the experience of Christians in Sudan and Indonesia, Ellul's pessimistic realism is well warranted. Dhimmitude is not merely something to be studied by historians; it still goes on wherever Islam gains an edge.

Are Christian and Islamic fundamentalism the same? It's hard to find a Christian fundamentalist in America who says slavery was righteous because slaves were kept alive. Muslims typically defend dhimmitude, however, by saying that Muslims could have expelled or killed Christians and Jews, but deserve credit for letting them live. (Of course, genocide against the inhabitants of conquered nations would have left Arabs with depopulated areas and not much likelihood of repopulating them.) Some also have said that their predecessors gave opportunities to the children of dhimmis by removing them from their Christian or Jewish parents and bringing them up in Islam. (That went along with the belief that all children are born Muslims and corrupted by parents.)

Other defenders of Islam have asserted that dhimmi status was better than anything offered Jews under Christianity. That is generally not true: For example, under Byzantine authority Jews could not purchase any property that the church had; under Islam they could purchase no property, period. Under the Byzantines, Jews could act as witnesses; not so under Islam. In any event, those who accepted dhimmi status, Bat Ye'or notes, were left with "no genuine rights," because under dhimmitude a person has no claim to any rights, only permission that could be rescinded.

In short, Islamic fundamentalism and Christian fundamentalism are worlds apart. Christian fundamentalists are sometimes nice people and sometimes not, but they can live at peace with their neighbors since all people have inalienable rights. Muslim fundamentalists are sometimes nice people and sometimes not, but to be Quranic strict constructionists, they and dhimmis can have only a temporary ceasefire. This is a huge difference that many journalists have irresponsibly overlooked. Some admit that they have not reported the truth, but say that if they had, they would be pouring gasoline on a fire. Some say their task is to help bring peace to all mankind. Some reporters from Christian backgrounds say that "stirring up trouble" by reporting about the warlike propensities of Islam would not be loving their neighbors.

TIME FOR TRUTH

I don't remember his name, but I do remember what a Kentucky Baptist preacher/weekly newspaper editor told me almost two decades ago. He had a police band radio and liked to go out with his camera when he heard that a drunk was being arrested. Unlike the paparazzi, he never chased anyone, but he did take photos of staggering citizens stopped by police, and then he put those pictures on his front page. The preacher told about a man who came to his office one day, pleading with him not to publish embarrassing photos of his brother. This man gave an emotion-grabbing reason for his request: "If you run those shots of Bubba, it'll just kill Mama." The editor replied, "Tell Bubba he better not drive drunk."

Did the preacher/editor lack love? Some—especially those who put bullet holes through his office window—said so. But the editor believed that if embarrassment could force a life-saving change in behavior, it would not be loving to look the other way. The same principle applies with other sins that we perceive, both in ourselves and others. We are not being kind to ourselves when we fool ourselves into thinking that wrong is right; nor are we loving others when we are not truthful. As the apostle Paul pointed out in his first letter to the troubled church in Corinth, "Love does not delight in evil but rejoices with the truth" (1 Cor. 13:6 NIV).

Paul himself rejoiced with the truth and fought against lies. He emphasized to the Ephesians the need for "speaking the truth in love," but one verse before that famous phrase in chapter 4 he criticized "the cunning and craftiness of men in their deceitful scheming" (Eph. 4:14 NIV). In case we still have any tendency to think that sugarcoating is next to godliness, Paul sums it up in Ephesians 4:25 NIV: "Therefore each of you must put off falsehood and speak truthfully to his neighbor, for we are all members of one body."

Christ certainly spoke the truth in love, but many of His statements were not sweet. In the Gospel of Matthew alone, He called His opponents "ferocious wolves," "vipers," "hypocrites," "blind fools," and so on. When Peter acted wrongly, Jesus said, "Get behind me, Satan." Nor were Christ's actions weak: He loved the moneychangers when he used a whip to drive them out of the temple. He loved

His neighbors enough to tell them the truth about their actions and their need to repent.

There is, of course, a big difference between God's inspired words and our words that may convey unrighteous anger. Insisting that love and truth go together does not give us a license to speak the truth spitefully. But the tendency among many Christians today is to lean in the opposite direction: Love rules, truth loiters behind. We forget that love and truth can be like sodium and chloride. Love without truth is mush, and truth without love can be poisonous. Sodium and chloride together make salt.

We desperately need salty journalists who are willing to explain that the God of the Bible is a far cry from the Islamic description of Allah as a just master who allows us to be his slaves—but not his children. Theological autocracy underlies human autocracy. Individuals who perceive themselves as sinless can amass a huge amount of power and are rarely willing to give it up by allowing elections or other expressions of popular will. Unable to defeat tyrants electorally, those in opposition turn to a terrorism that destroys whatever good has been accomplished. Joni Mitchell sang, "You don't know what you've got till it's gone./ Take paradise and put up a parking lot." Societies with Christian heritages are hardly paradises—Christianity itself shows the ravaging effects of sin—but their superiority to those lacking that teaching is evident in area after area.

We desperately need salty journalists who understand that God as described in the Bible is a God of freedom, properly understood. The one true God knows our sinful frames and is grieved by our disobedience. He is portrayed as a husband who feels pain because of an unfaithful wife or as a father brokenhearted by his children's rebellion. He did what was necessary to reconcile God and man without violating His standards of holiness. He adopts us into His family.

5

EXPLAINING
CHRISTIANITY

In recent years U.S. daily newspapers haven't shown much appreciation for biblical belief, but since the 9/11 disasters many have been praising the utility of religion generally. The *Austin American-Statesman*'s September 8, 2002, front-page headline was typical: "When a nation needed comfort, religion was there." (And when a nation needs comfort food, meatloaf is there.) The *Statesman* continued, "Many instinctively called upon religious faith. Others found traditional religion lacking and sought alternative means of comfort through yoga, meditation, or acts of charity."

These comments show that many reporters equate "religion" with the pursuit of comfort rather than the pursuit of truth. Marxism has faltered around the world, but Karl Marx's depiction of religion as "the opiate of the masses" has sunk deeply into journalistic roots. Neither this article nor many others had any recognition that Christianity does indeed bring comfort but stands or falls on the issue of truth—for, as Paul told the Corinthians, if Christianity is not true, "we are of all people most to be pitied."

Two elements—truth and love—distinguish Christianity from all other religions. As the last chapter noted, those who stand for Christ need the support of both in order to persevere, just as Moses needed to have his arms supported by Aaron and Hur. In the movie *A Few Good Men*, Lt. Kaffe (Tom Cruise) says, "I want the truth," and

Col. Jessup (Jack Nicholson) responds, "You can't handle the truth." But in life what really harms us is not the truth but the lie that all is well even as the disease is pervasive.

When a body is overrun with cancer, it's important for the soul of the soon-to-be-deceased and for the plans of a spouse and children to handle the truth and not hide from it. On lesser matters as well, honesty counts. I typically tell journalism students on the first day of a course that they need a real friend who will honestly tell them that their writing stinks, when it does (and will use direct, one-syllable words to say so). One poetry professor has his students criticize each other's poetry, but he also tells them that of all the people in the classroom, only one, himself, is paid not to lie to them. Likewise every Christian should tell the truth because Jesus has already paid for each of us to do so.

So what is the truth? Christianity emphasizes love, not the smarmy kind, but the robust love of a father for his son. Christianity emphasizes the good news that God came to earth to suffer with us and die for us. Secularists sometimes say that's a sweet story but just a fantasy. They generally have two major objections. One is that the odds against the Christian story being true are so great that belief in it takes an incredible amount of faith. A second objection is that key doctrines don't make logical sense. Let's look at those two concerns, not with the evangelistic supposition that one person can convince another to become a Christian—only God can do that—but in the belief that the Bible is true and that all people should be told the truth.

AN ODD STORY'S ODDS

Christ's virgin birth and His resurrection from the dead were astonishing occurrences, sure, but other events have been far more improbable. To name a few—that an orderly universe exists at all, that earth is a place where life can exist, and that complex organs such as eyes have emerged.

Biblically, we know that the odds of these things happening apart from God are zero. Even from a materialist perspective, the odds against our being here are enormous. John Blanchard's book *Does God Believe in Atheists?* provides some of the numbers: He notes that Roger Penrose, who helped to develop black hole theories, estimated as one in 100 billion to the 123rd power the odds of a big bang producing by accident an orderly universe as opposed to chaos. Big bang theorists argue that the universe one second after its purported start had to expand at a rate rapid enough to keep in check the gravitational attraction of galaxies. Stephen Hawking has noted that if the rate of expansion had been smaller by an infinitesimal amount, the universe would have collapsed.

Blanchard quotes useful analogies about the likelihood of the universe allowing for the existence of life. What's the likelihood of hitting a target an inch wide on the other side of the observable universe? How about expecting a pole vaulter's pole to remain standing, poised on its tip, for centuries following his vault? Of course, even if the universe by chance came out right for human existence, we would need a livable home in space. Earth's size, distance from the sun, and rotational speed had to be just right. We need the air above not only for breathing but to protect us from cosmic rays and meteorites. We need light (but not much ultraviolet), heat (but not too much), and so on.

Does Christ's resurrection seem incredible? What about the origin of life? A chance of one out of 1,000,000,000,000,000 is considered a virtual impossibility, but when DNA co-discoverer Francis Crick calculated the possibility of a simple protein sequence of 200 amino acids (much simpler than a DNA molecule) originating spontaneously, his figure was 10 with 260 zeroes after it.

Those who remember a past fad will appreciate British scientist Fred Hoyle's view of the odds against evolved life. "Anyone with even a nodding acquaintance with the Rubik cube," he wrote, "will concede the near impossibility of a solution being obtained by a blind person moving the cube faces at random. Now imagine 10 to the fiftieth power blind persons (standing shoulder to shoulder, these would more than fill our entire planetary system) each with a scrambled Rubik cube . . . simultaneously arriving at the solved form."

Hoyle's best-known analogy is a tornado in a junkyard taking all the pieces of metal lying there and turning them into a Boeing 747. It would be amazing but possible for two pieces to be naturally welded together, and then two pieces more in a later whirlwind, but production of even a simple organic molecule would require all of the pieces to come together at one time. Three decades ago Frank Salisbury of Utah State University described the odds this way: Imagine 100 million trillion planets, each with an ocean with lots of DNA fragments that reproduce one million times per second, with a mutation occurring each time. In four billion years it would still take trillions of universes to produce a single gene—if they got lucky.

So the really odd story is that we are here at all. Since those odds have not inhibited defenders of macro-evolution during recent decades, Christians who are ridiculed for adhering to the less unlikely possibility of Christ's birth and resurrection should not be embarrassed. Christians know that time plus chance did not lead to our present situation, but it is a great encouragement to Christians to see how infinitesimal is the possibility of the materialist scenario. Christians should confront atheists with this evidence, show them the fallacy of their worldview, and leave them in despair, for it's at the point of despair that God often seems to regenerate minds.

True believers in Darwinism might better be depicted as true believers in avoiding at all costs the alternative. The late science-fiction writer Isaac Asimov acknowledged that he did not "have the information to prove that God doesn't exist," but "emotionally, I'm an atheist." So here's a key question: Do unbelievers want to know whether Christ rose from the dead, or are they emotionally committed to closed eyes and ears? Aldous Huxley wrote of the philosopher trying "to prove that there is no valid reason why he personally should not do as he wants to do. . . . We don't know because we don't want to know."

Those who do want to know should investigate thoroughly, without assuming that the Resurrection could not have happened. If God created the entire world out of nothing, the Resurrection (or a virgin birth or parting the Red Sea or having the sun stand still without the earth being destroyed) is an easy task.

HONESTY VERSUS PROPAGANDA

The revelation contained within the four gospel accounts is the reasonable culmination and logical successor of the Old Testament. We could even put the Old Testament to New Testament flow in terms taken from newspapers and movies: cover-up, communication, cliffhanger, and crime.

The *cover-up* seems surpassingly evident to Christians and—given the failures of Darwinism—increasingly hard for even atheists to ignore. We see all around us evidence that the world was intelligently designed. When we ignore the giant headlines in the sky that proclaim, "There is a Creator," and the whispering in our own brain, "There is a Creator," we are entering into a cover-up bigger than Watergate, Whitewater, and many other scandals piled one on another.

The *communication* would be a big story only if it weren't there. It would be strange if a Creator who gave man the ability to talk and listen and read would not communicate with His desperately needy creatures. An inquiring mind would expect God to provide a written record of some kind, one that would last. Lay aside the ancient myths of nations that died out—where are Hittite scriptures now?—and there are only three main candidate religions, all two millennia or more old: Buddhism, Hinduism, and Judeo-Christianity. Add Islam, and it's not too hard to check out the scriptures of the final four ourselves.

The *cliffhanger* is evident to readers of mysteries. The Old

Testament's powerful majesty moves many hearts, but its ending leaves many unanswered questions. The Old Testament contains enormous specific detail about the need for and establishment of a sacrificial system, and then shows how that system proved inadequate in changing lives. But would God end the sacrificial system in A.D. 70 (with the destruction of the temple) and let His means of atonement disappear without providing something to take its place? The last books of the Old Testament indicate enormous yearning for a Messiah but offer no resolution.

The *crime* in the sequel known as the New Testament is the sensational story of an innocent man judicially murdered. Other elements of the story include a brilliant and obviously sane man making crazy-sounding claims to be the Son of God and then suffering a gruesome execution. After that comes even more astounding news: Although the man's corpse was wrapped in a burial cloth and placed in a police-secured sealed tomb, many reliable sources reported that He rose from the dead and that they walked, talked, and ate with Him. Mass hallucination? A conspiracy of misreporting? Or a strange-but-true story?

Some secularists show appreciation for a sensational saga like that, but then they ask other skeptical questions: Couldn't Paul have been psychologically ill when he was writing his letters? Couldn't the Gospels have been written later on by brilliant liars who read the Old Testament prophecies and then invented Jesus to fit them? For that matter, weren't those prophecies produced after the fact, as German "higher critics" of the nineteenth century insisted?

Much of that "higher criticism" has been brought low by research that has pushed the writing of the Gospels and Epistles back to within three decades of the time when the events took place. But that still does not guarantee that the events are as described. Parson Weems wrote his biographies of George Washington in 1800 and 1806 (Washington died in 1799) but made up stories to make his hero look good. He wanted the father of the United States to be an ethical giant; so he had Washington confessing to the cherry tree incident and others. Why couldn't the Bible writers have shown their heroes to be always honest from childhood through old age?

Bible writers could have, as writers of other ancient religious scriptures did. But one indication that they were truth-tellers was their willingness to cover lots of bad news in a manner remarkably different from other ancient scribes. In most ancient scriptures, founders of religions are demi-gods. Biblical writers, however, often portrayed their giants as ethical pygmies. Noah, recently saved from death by flood, got passed-out drunk. Abraham, fearing for his life, may have been ready to pimp his wife. Jacob was a deceiver, Samson a muscular twit, David an adulterer who covered up that act by having a loyal captain killed. If the Bible's goal was propaganda, its writers were incompetent, and yet that's not what readers moved by surpassing beauty tend to infer.

Furthermore, the "broken windows" theory of crime prevention—sweat the small things because cities that allow minor property destruction soon see their rape and murder statistics rising—works in determining scriptural credibility as well. Since the Bible throughout claims that it is God's communication with man, factual inaccuracies uncovered through the work of archeologists could torpedo that claim. Material that's accurate in its specific detail attests to the reliability of the whole.

Repeatedly, biblical accounts considered mythical by some nineteenth-century scholars have gained new archeological support. As John Blanchard points out, famous German scholar Julius Wellhausen considered the Genesis story of Abraham rescuing Lot "simply impossible," but archeological research now shows all the details of that story to have been accurate. The conventional wisdom was that the city of Ur from which Abraham supposedly came did not exist, but excavations now show Ur to have been an advanced city. For a long time some archeologists viewed the Sodom and Gomorrah story as fiction, but excavations at Tell

Mardikh uncovered tablets mentioning both those cities as having been destroyed.

The nineteenth-century view was that Moses would probably have been illiterate; so someone else must have written the five books ascribed to him. But historians now recognize that the Egyptian upper class was highly literate. Scholars at one point said that the Hittites described in the Bible did not exist, nor did rulers such as Belshazzar of Babylon or Sargon of Assyria. Archeologists now have records of all those civilizations and reigns.

The Old Testament refers by name to about forty kings during the 1,600-year period from 2000 to 400 B.C. If those names were inaccurate or out of order, that would also be a strike against biblical reliability. But Princeton's Robert Dick Wilson, who knew twenty-six ancient languages and dialects and so could read just about all that remains from the ancient Near East, came to a different conclusion. He wrote, in *A Scientific Investigation of the Old Testament*, that "No stronger evidence for the substantial evidence of the Old Testament record could possibly be imagined than the collection of kings. Mathematically, it is one chance in [750 with 21 zeroes after it] that this accuracy is mere circumstance."

DATING THE NEW TESTAMENT

The New Testament provides the same combination of political incorrectness and accuracy. Just as the Old Testament had bad news about the founders of the faith, the New Testament reports the cowardice of Peter the apostle and others. Someone producing a public relations brochure in ancient Rome would never have given women such vital roles in the founding of a religion—women as the first witnesses of the empty tomb would add to suspicion as to whether Christ truly rose from the dead.

The New Testament displays the work of honest writers trying to tell what occurred, regardless of consequences. The gospel accounts show Jesus claiming equality with God the Father, the ability to forgive sins, and existence before Abraham (Mark 2:5-7; John 5:17-18; John 8:58). As C. S. Lewis famously put it, if this self-assessment isn't true, Jesus was either a malicious liar or a raving lunatic. Yet many people believed He was neither, and His sayings don't suggest either of those alternatives. Furthermore, Jesus showed that He was God through His miracles, particularly the feedings of 4,000 and 5,000. We have faith healers today who try to show that they can imitate Christ, but we have no faith-feeders who take loaves and fish and feed thousands of people. No magicians, not even those with superb sleight of hand, not even David Copperfield and assorted television stars, have tried that.

Nineteenth-century skeptics proposed that New Testament books were written generations after the events they describe. And yet look how the authors displayed precision in specific detail. Description in the book of Acts of Roman legal practice, Jewish synagogue customs, the social significance of magicians, and so forth have been shown authentic in every detail, and that gives the entire story the ring of truth. The accurate use of official titles is particularly impressive, since Roman titles were far from standard, and writers a century later would not have known that some officials were called tetrarchs in Galilee, politarchs at Thessalonica, asiarchs in Ephesus, proconsuls in Corinth and Cyprus, and protos in Malta. The New Testament writers got the story details right.

Here's a rough parallel: Naval archeologists who had plans, memoirs, and period drawings thought they knew just about the whole story of the *USS Monitor*, the famous Civil War ironclad. But now that a $14 million project has lifted most of the ship into daylight after its 140 years at the bottom of the sea, the experts have been surprised to find undocumented braces on the gun turret and mustard bottles where the crew ate. If we found in some musty library a document asserting that the crew had added some braces and braced their taste buds by pouring mustard on otherwise inedible biscuits, we would be much more likely to give that manuscript an origin stamp of 1870 rather than 1970.

To get specific details right, writers have to be on the scene or in contact with onlookers and officials. Those wanting to disparage New Testament books face a dilemma. If critics date them early, credibility goes up. It's hard to turn history into myth when not much time has elapsed and eyewitnesses are still on the scene. If they date them late, the existence of specific detail makes that dating incredible. Overall, it appears that at least the first three Gospels—Matthew, Mark, and Luke—were composed within thirty years of the death of Christ while many eyewitnesses to the events described were still alive. Paul's epistles and the book of Acts were all written during the '50s and early '60s, since Paul appears to have been put to death in Emperor Nero's persecution of A.D. 64.

BLAME THE COPYISTS?

Accurate specific detail undercuts the case of critics, but they have one more way out. Say the documents do have early dates, but as they were copied, the copyists kept the factual framework and distorted the doctrines to conform to their own prejudices. After all, we do not have the original manuscripts. They are long gone. No one tried to preserve scrolls hundreds of years old, and there was no way to do so except in terrible desert conditions, since moisture is the enemy of parchment. (Look at the climate control we need to preserve the Declaration of Independence.) Old copies were burned or buried. Until 1947 the earliest existing manuscript of the Old Testament that we still have, called the Masoretic Text, was dated around A.D. 900.

In that year, though, people found 2,000-year-old scrolls hidden in a desert cave near Israel's Dead Sea. The Dead Sea Scrolls contained portions from the book of Isaiah and other Bible books that are virtually identical to the ones we have now. That means the copying over the years was very accurate; only a few verses are questionable, usually because of small variations in words and spelling that do not throw any doctrines into question. As the historian Flavius Josephus wrote in the first century A.D., "although long ages have now passed, no one has ventured even to add, or to remove, or to alter a syllable."

Copying records show how hard scribes worked to have accurate transmission. Old Testament copyists from A.D. 100 to 500 wrote exactly thirty letters on each line of parchment, and every letter had to be written while the scribe referred to the original manuscript; writing from memory was banned. For easy checking each book ended on a prescribed line on the parchment and was checked and rechecked. Frederic Kenyon, the British Museum's director and principal librarian, put it this way: "The same extreme care which was devoted to the transcription of manuscripts is also at the bottom of the disappearance of the earlier copies. When a manuscript had been copied with the exactitude prescribed by the Talmud, and had been duly verified, it was accepted as authentic and regarded as being of equal value with any other copy. If all were equally correct, age gave no advantage to a manuscript."

As for the New Testament, 25,000 manuscript copies of all or part of it exist. That compares with ten copies of the work of Roman historian Tacitus (born in A.D. 52), seven copies of writings by Pliny the Younger (born in A.D. 61), and nothing completely trustworthy about Alexander the Great (born in 356 B.C.). Experts say that 50 to 150 variants in all these copies of the Bible could make for some change in meaning. Not a single one, though, affects an article of faith or duty whose validity is unclear from many other passages and scriptural teaching generally. Homer's *Iliad*—653 manuscript copies of it exist—has twenty times more textual questions about it than the Bible has. As scholar F. F. Bruce wrote, "There is no body of ancient literature in the world which enjoys such a wealth of good textual attestation as the New Testament."

The earliest existing manuscript of famous Roman writers such as Pliny and Tacitus is 750 years old, but the earliest New Testament manuscripts we have are partial copies dating to a century after their original composition. Our earliest Plato and Aristotle manuscripts are hundreds of years after the fact. Frederick Kenyon of the British Museum says of books from the ancient world, "In no other case is the interval of time between the composition of the book and the date of the earliest extant manuscripts so short as that of the New Testament." Overall, much as traditional and higher criticism of the Bible both fall short, so does the textual critique.

COLORING OUTSIDE THE LINES

One argument against the Genesis account of Adam and Eve is that other ancient scriptures contain stories of man's disobedience and God's punishment. An argument against the account of Noah and the great flood is that other ancient peoples also have flood stories. An argument against Christ's death and resurrection is that other ancient cultures also told of a dying god coming back to life. Cynical journalists contend that the biblical accounts are no more valid than crime-reporting formulas.

Of course, the reason other flood stories might exist is that the Flood happened. The reason other cultures might tell of a dying god coming back to life is that implanted deep in the human heart is the notion that this would be a wonderful thing for a god to do. No ancient religion other than Christianity shows how death and resurrection bridged the chasm between God's holiness and man's sinfulness. A further indication of biblical authenticity is that the writers often departed from formulas, not only in depicting sinful heroes but in coloring outside the lines; someone only desiring credibility for a story would be unlikely to include evidence and views that hurt his cause. But the Bible does so repeatedly.

One example is views of women. Classical scholars have mused about "the glory that was Greece," but ancient Greece was glorious neither for slaves nor those near-slaves known as wives. An Athenian wife was not allowed to eat with her husband's guests nor leave the house without male escort. Spartan women probably had more freedom but were still kept under lock and key, according to the second-century biographer Plutarch. Greek men viewed women as inferior at birth; as in China today, Greek baby girls suffered infanticide far more often than boys. Greeks viewed women as inferior during childhood: Non-slave Athenian boys went to school; girls did not. They viewed women as inferior during adulthood: "Evil are they and guileful of purpose, with impure hearts," the great fifth-century dramatist Aeschylus had his chorus declare.

In Rome, similarly, men had complete authority over their wives, even to the point of being able to divorce them if they went outside without a veil and to kill them if they committed adultery. Roman men commonly spoke scornfully about women. The historian Tacitus wrote that women are by nature cruel, and the humorist Juvenal thought that women are so low that "there is nothing a woman will not permit herself to do." The best way for a new religious idea to win support was to exclude women from any meaningful participation, except as shrine prostitutes.

Christianity opposed this age-old pattern. Jesus set the example by speaking respectfully to and teaching a Samaritan woman and two Jewish women. He let women be His followers. He appeared before several women after His resurrection. The apostle Paul wrote respectfully of women who were leaders in pulling together Christians in Colossae, Ephesus, Philippi, and Laodicea. He instructed Christian men to be willing to die for their wives as Christ died for the church.

IS THE BIBLE ILLOGICAL?

Let's say evidence such as that just offered overcomes the first typical secularist objection that the odds against Christianity being true are too great. There remains the issue of the particular doctrines taught. Do they make sense? Of course, given our limited understanding, they cannot make sense to us the way they make sense to God. But since man is made in God's image, we should be able to, in a fallen and sinful way, think some of God's thoughts after Him. His work in our eyes is like that of a mathematical genius developing a complex theorem on a pane of glass, except more so—but at least we can see that the math whiz is using numbers and letters.

The first way that the Bible insults the logic of many secularists is that it shows one couple or individual—first Adam and Eve and later Jesus—changing everything about our lives through decisions they made. That original sin could affect others or that Christ could later substitute His atonement for ours does not go over well with those taught as students that each person must do his own work. Why should we be so injured by the work of another and then so helped?

Let's go back to man's beginning. The Bible says that people were created to live in a Garden of Eden that God made for them. God offered plenty of time for challenging intellectual work (studying animals, nature, and the world God created, and then naming things rightly) and pleasant physical breaks (tending a garden that produced great flowers and food, not thorns). We don't know what else God would have provided in the unlikely situation that Adam and Eve ran out of interesting things to do. We do know that Adam and Eve had no good reason to balance what God was saying against what someone else was saying.

The problem, though, is that Adam and Eve saw themselves as neutral observers, able to decide between good and evil. They had free will, and they chose wrongly, with consequences for themselves and all their posterity, which includes us. Adam represented us, in one sense, as a president at times represents the nation. We're stuck with some of his decisions whether we like them or not. Or we could say that Eve represented us as our parents and grandparents represent us. If a child's mother drinks heavily, he has no choice in the matter of whether he will have fetal alcohol syndrome. (Lest we blame others for our own afflictions, we should note that we all have the choice Adam and Eve had—whether to obey God or disregard His promises and warnings—and who can say that we do any better than the first couple?)

All of us have also been affected by another decision, that of Christ, whose punishment substitutes for ours. That's really not too hard to understand. After all, Charles Dickens (*A Tale of Two Cities*) and other novelists have written of an innocent person dying for another. Maybe we don't like to think that one person living long ago could affect our lives so much—but keep in mind how much we owe to each of our ancestors over the past several thousand years. Had any one of hundreds changed his actions in any one of an infinite number of ways, thus affecting (among other things) whether and when we were conceived, not one of us would be the person he is. So none of us is autonomous even in the smallest degree. Once we accept that and recognize that we are ruled either by chance or by God's providence, we lose illusions of autonomy and are ready to have either faith in God or faith in nothingness. Christians should show atheists that the only choice is God or despair.

THE LOGIC OF SUFFERING

Some secularists have suffered much or seen their friends suffer. They ask, "Couldn't an all-powerful God prevent suffering? Wouldn't an all-loving God prevent it?" C. S. Lewis, however, noted (in *The Problem of Pain*), "The problem of reconciling human suffering with the existence of a God who loves is insoluble only so long as we attach a trivial meaning to the word 'love.'" God, Lewis observed, loves us enough to want to change our focus from the immediate to the long range, even to eternity. A theocentric view turns the humanistically meaningless upside down. One well-known Christian writer and speaker, Joni Eareckson Tada, was immersed in meaninglessness until she dove into shallow water and broke her neck. Her paralysis eventually led her to God. Her testimony has inspired millions of others.

In many worldviews, suffering arises out of bad luck or because of a person's fault, and neither of those reasons brings honor in its train. But in Christianity, suffering results from neither chance nor karma, but it is part of God's plan, generally for reasons we don't know but can later on, at times, partly fathom. Dorothy Sayers wrote (in *The Whimsical Christian*) that understanding the honor of being chosen to suffer for a great cause gives Christianity "its enormous advantage over every other religion in the world. It is the only religion that gives value to evil and suffering." It does that by affirming the reality of evil, the need to confront it, and the opportunity to wrench good out of it as Christ did when He suffered and died for all who believe in Him.

Do mysteries remain? Of course. Theologian J. I. Packer observed (in *Knowing God*) that none of us, as human beings, will ever gain the wisdom we need to answer the hardest questions about suffering and death. We sometimes think that if we only study enough, and maybe pray enough, that God will present us with the big picture of how the details of suffering add up. But the way of biblical wisdom, Packer points out, is to believe "that the inscrutable God of providence is the wise and gracious God of creation and redemption." That's where faith comes in. Without faith, we may believe that a schizophrenic God creates beauty but also suffering. With faith, we can work hard at whatever God calls us to do for as long as we can, enjoying the gifts bestowed on us and not going crazy because we don't have more or because we lost what cannot be regained. Is this consolation amid suffering? Not immediately, but God created time, and time, properly used, applies balm to wounds.

Without a Christian understanding, people with a social conscience are anxious, not recognizing the quality of God's mercy. In Leo Tolstoy's great short story "What Men Live By," an angel is distressed when twin babies whose father has been killed in a logging accident are about to lose their mother as well. "Little children cannot live without father or mother," the angel tells God, and refuses to take the mother's life. Sent to earth helpless and wingless to learn some important lessons, the angel eventually realizes that men, women, and even orphans live not by human or even angelic considerations of necessity, but by God's mercy.

A decade ago the problems of babies exposed to cocaine while in the womb seemed impossible to overcome. Some nurses reacted as the angel did, doubting God: Not only were crack babies off to a tough early start, but they would lead lives of mental disability or very slow development. But new studies tell a story of God's mercy although they do not even mention God. The experts now say that these children, given a good, secure environment rather than one infested with drugs and general parental instability, regularly overcome the effects of maternal cocaine exposure.

God's mercy is apparent when we choose to look for it. Hurricanes and severe storms are called "acts of God," but we often ignore the far more numerous acts of God that keep us alive day by day. We read reports of terrible auto accidents, but we never know how many just as horrible were barely averted. We see international mercies as well but quickly tend to take them for granted. How often do we ponder the amazing end of the Soviet Union over a decade ago or the non-use of nuclear weapons for over half a century?

Some secularists recognize that a God angry with sin would demean Himself and miseducate us if, like a fairy godmother, He were to wave a wand and eliminate its consequences. They still question the legitimacy of that anger. Some ask, "Didn't God create the problem? Why didn't He create people unable to rebel against Him?" We might also ask, "Why is there news? Why do we have man-bites-dog stories, pennant races in baseball, and blind dates?" We are part of a great story with lots of twists and turns; if indeed we are actors in this enormous drama, we are actors making up our lines as we go, not knowing how any scene or act will turn out.

One way to explain this is to understand that for God all times are the present: He knows and ordains past and future while we know only a little about the past and nothing about the future.

Keeping that fact in mind, we can jump off from historian Herbert Butterfield's view of God as a composer repeatedly revising his music because the orchestra playing it is incompetent. If we say that God is surprised by incompetence or is at the mercy of the performers, rushing to revise the score so the symphony will end up where He wants it, we are underestimating God's power and not saying what the Bible says. But God does not operate in time; He already has finished the entire score, writing in the idiosyncrasies of the clarinetist and the tumbles of the tuba player. He has foreordained the future without limiting human freedom because for God the future is no different than the past.

Christians find the idea that God is in charge not only true but comforting. (Otherwise, imagine the torment after an accident: *If I hadn't delayed my son by giving him a second helping of pie, he wouldn't have been in that accident a few minutes later.*) G. K. Chesterton wrote that the doctrine of original sin is a cheerful concept since within it suffering, failure, and inadequacy arise neither from blind chance nor necessarily as part of punishment, but as the common lot of humanity.

What makes all this work is the experience of Christ, who knew what it was to be unjustly tortured and abandoned, to endure overwhelming loss, and to be unjustly killed. The ancient Greeks distinguished between *gnosis* (intellectual knowledge) and *epignosis* (intimate understanding drawn from personal experience). Regardless of how well made some travel videos are, virtual travel is not the real thing. I've never seen a photo or video that conveys the full magnificence of the Grand Canyon or a great glacier. I can view a major league ballpark on television many times, but until I've been there myself, I don't really comprehend its nooks and crannies. That is the difference between *gnosis* and *epignosis*.

Christians also know that God is real and that Allah is a human construct. But if an Allah really did exist in a parallel universe, he could not be omniscient, since complete knowledge requires *epignosis* along with *gnosis*. Since for God all times are the present, He had the knowledge of what it was to experience life as a human being even before the creation of the earth. God has *gnosis* and *epignosis* concerning the human condition, but the theoretical Allah has only *gnosis*.

Peggy Noonan wrote in 2001 in her *Wall Street Journal* column about a husband and wife swimming in the ocean when "from nowhere came a shark. The shark went straight for the woman, opened its jaws. Do you know what the man did? He punched the shark in the head. . . . So the shark let go of his wife and went straight for him. And it killed him. The wife survived to tell the story of what her husband had done. He had tried to deck the shark. I told my friends: That's what a wonderful man is, a man who will try to deck the shark." Christians believe that all of us should be shark bait because of our sin. If God were to ignore our sin simply by destroying the shark from afar, we could thank Him and venerate Him, but would we love Him? As it is, Christians say, *What a wonderful God, coming to earth to deck the shark.*

THE LOGIC OF DEATH

The ultimate objective test of a religion at this time is whether it holds up under rigorous analysis and examination of the evidence. The ultimate subjective test is whether it holds up under the most rigorous test of life, which is the coming of death. John Calvin made the understanding of death a milestone of sanctification: "If anyone cannot set his mind at ease by disregarding death, that man should know that he has not yet gone far enough in the faith of Christ."

So how do we stand? Today's secular death ethicists say they're on top of the subject, but they need to develop pitcher Jim Bouton's self-awareness: "You think you're gripping the baseball, only to find that it's gripping you." Medical advances make dying physically less savage now. Yet emotional frigidity cuts as deep as an ice pick. Hospices provide a good alternative to death in hospitals, but changing the physical environment does not necessarily help us to master death spiritually and psychologically. Writers to "Dear Abby" for

years offered sad reports of death-fear mastering pleasant environ-
ments. For example, "Grieving in Orange, Texas" wrote of how
patients "are scared to death, and no medicine I have seen completely
eradicates that pain."

For those without hope, no medicine can eliminate the fear and
pain. Minnesota pastor John Piper, in his book *Future Grace*, writes of
two skydivers, both free-falling at the same speed. One has a
parachute, and one does not. Only the person who knows he has a
parachute to open will enjoy the sensation. To develop the metaphor
further, the other person may conclude that parachutes are imaginary,
that he should put the impending impact out of his mind, that new
medical knowledge is sinking the ground by a few feet—but he is still
likely to be miserable.

Christians have the advantage of knowing that there are
parachutes and the responsibility to tell others that parachutes are
available and should be deployed. This is not mere theoretical talk;
for nearly 2,000 years Christians have faced death with sadness at
times but not despair. The apostle Paul argued that the prospect of
resurrection shatters the fear of death: "Where, O death, is your victory? Where, O death, is your sting?" (1 Cor. 15:55 NIV). Someday
death will die as well: Paul wrote, "The last enemy to be destroyed is
death" (1 Cor. 15:26 NIV).

This belief made a practical difference during Christianity's early
centuries. Romans traditionally buried the dead at night outside the
city walls, partly for reasons of health but largely because of repug-
nance and a desire to keep the dead out of sight and mind. But
Christians did not think of death with loathing, and they kept burials
close, with bodies placed next to or under churches. Christian funer-
als took place during the day whenever possible to make it clear that
the dead person was entering not into darkness but into bright eternal
life. Mourners carried torches before the dead not for light, but
because Romans did that when a victorious general had a triumph.

This custom spread throughout the empire. In A.D. 407, when

church leader John Chrysostom died, his body was taken by ship to Constantinople. So many persons holding lamps came out in boats that the "sea was covered with lamps." Over the next millennium many were influenced to adhere to Christianity by observing, as author T. R. Glover would point out: "Christians out-die pagans and the resurrection of Christ is the reason."

When poet John Donne was dying in 1631, he asked his lawyer to conclude all legal work related to Donne's estate before "Saturday next, for after that day he would not mix his thoughts with any thing that concerned the world." Donne lived on for several days after that, "happy to have nothing to do but die." In the last hour of his last day, Donne had visions of heaven and said as his final words, "I were miserable if I might not die. Thy Kingdom come, Thy Will be done."

Others also noted Christian conduct as death approached. People who thought man was merely another animal often had last-minute panic attacks. Bible commentator Matthew Henry wrote that "death to a godly man is like a fair gale of wind to convey him to the heavenly country; but to a wicked man it is an east wind, a storm, a tempest, that hurries him away in confusion and amazement, to destruction." Methodist pioneer John Wesley stated simply, "Our people die well." British essayist Joseph Addison's dying words in 1719 were: "See in what peace a Christian can die." Hymns even conveyed a sense of excitement. The fourth stanza of an Easter favorite, Charles Wesley's "Christ the Lord Is Risen Today" (1739), begins: "Soar we now where Christ has led." The fourth stanza of "Rock of Ages" (1776) has a similar image: "When mine eyelids close in death,/ When I soar to worlds unknown."

Everyone needs to understand the triumph in Christian death prior to old age, for as Michigan church pastor Robert Zagore put it, "A deathbed is a hard place to teach the faith. It is much better learned day by day, week by week." He wrote of an elderly woman in his church: "When I last saw her, she was in the hospital bed she would not leave alive. The last words I spoke to her were 3,400 years older

than she. . . . 'The Lord bless you and keep you. The Lord make his
face shine on you and be gracious to you. The Lord lift up his coun-
tenance on you and give you peace.' She knew He would. The last
word I heard her say, I overheard her say to God: 'Amen.'"

Contrast this with the experience of Kirk Bains, a highly successful stock speculator who was stricken with cancer and told by top
specialists that nothing could be done for him. Physician Jerome
Groopman, in *The Measure of Our Days*, tells how Bains came to him
and pleaded for treatment with an experimental procedure: "Cook up
some new magic. Make me a guinea pig. I take risks all the time.
That's my business. I won't sue you."

Groopman writes that he always tried "to learn the scope of religious feeling, the ties of the patient and his family to faith. God,
whether positive, negative, or null, is an essential factor in the equation
of dying." Bains replied, "I'm not a long-term investor. I like quick
returns. I don't believe in working for dividends paid in heaven."

The night before the radical surgery, Bains was troubled, telling
Groopman, "I know this is my last chance, and I'll probably die, and
after death . . . it's just nothingness. . . . No time. No place. No form.
I don't ask for heaven. I'd take hell. Just to be." The surgery was successful, and the cancer went into remission—but only for four
months. When it came back and Bains had an initial radiation treatment, Groopman visited him and said, "I'm sorry the magic didn't
work longer."

Bains replied, "You shouldn't feel sorry. There was no reason to
live anyway. . . . You read newspapers? . . . I don't read newspapers
anymore. I don't know how to. Or why I should. Newspapers used
to be a gold mine for me. They're filled with what to you looks like
disconnected bits of information. A blizzard in the Midwest, the
immigration debate in California . . . information for deals and com-
modity trading. . . . And when I went into remission I couldn't read
the papers because my deals and trades seemed pointless. Pointless
because I was a short-term investor. I had no patience for the long

term. I had no interest in creating something, not a product in business or a partnership with a person. And now I have no equity. No dividends coming in. Nothing to show in my portfolio."

Bains concluded, "How do you like my great epiphany? No voice of God or holy star but a newspaper left unread in its wrapper. . . . The remission meant nothing because it was too late to relive my life. I once asked for hell. Maybe God made this miracle to have me know what it will feel like." Groopman writes that he felt "the crushing weight of Kirk's burden" because "there is no more awful death than to die with regret, feeling that you have lived a wasted life—death delivering this shattering final sentence on your empty soul."

THE IMPORTANCE OF BELIEF

Some secularists I have talked with have great trouble with ideas of hell or of God's vengeance for—as one put it—"merely having the wrong ideas." And yet many do hope for particular kinds of vengeance. For example, David Baerwald, an Austin singer-songwriter on the political left, ten years ago put the following epigraph on his highly politicized album *Triage*: "This record is dedicated to Dean Acheson, Paul Nitze, John J. McCloy, John Foster Dulles, Allen Dulles, Henry Kissinger, James Baker III, and George Bush in the sincere hope that there is a God and that He is vengeful beyond all comprehension."

One Jewish person I greatly respect wrote to me after the 9/11 attacks when people were speculating on God's vengeance in regard to terrorists, abortionists, or others. He wrote, "I know that my God visited plagues on Egypt but wonder whether His affirmative vengeance can't be reserved for people who murder and enslave rather than those who merely lead self-referential, sybaritic lives and fail to acknowledge His existence?"

People disagree on the definition of evil and on what should be punished, but just about everyone would like God to punish some evildoers in some way. Some who believe in the God of the Bible think He lets evildoers fall into the pit they have dug and does not give them a push. That's the suggestion of a commandment such as "Honor your father and your mother, that your days may be long" (Exod. 20:12 ESV). Those who abort children and push euthanasia for their parents should not be surprised when they themselves receive a short good-bye.

But God also commands, "You shall not take the name of the LORD your God in vain, for the LORD will not hold him guiltless who takes his name in vain" (Exod. 20:7 ESV). He calls Himself "a jealous God, visiting the iniquity of the fathers on the children to the third and the fourth generation of those who hate me" (v. 5). That certainly sounds like active rather than passive enforcement. (We've certainly seen the truth of this commandment in Russia where children suffer now because decisions made by Communist grandparents and great-grandparents led to social and economic havoc.)

Maybe God is so explicit in those commandments because He knows that our tendency is to look at consequences rather than underlying ideas—and in doing so to underestimate the importance of belief in Him. Asked to name one of the Ten Commandments, most of us mention ones such as "You shall not murder" or "You shall not commit adultery." Those later commandments come without explanation. Just as the Declaration of Independence begins, "We hold these truths to be self-evident," so God apparently expects us to understand without being told why stealing and lying are wrong. But the initial commandments are different. God tells us what will happen when we mess up.

Many people think it's right for God to take vengeance on murderers but not atheists. That seems logical—why punish people for expressing ideas? But I think of how Abraham Lincoln dealt with Ohio Congressman Clement Vallandigham, a handsome and gifted speaker who in 1863 told thousands in his state that they should not support the Union in the Civil War. Lincoln ordered that the congressman be delivered to the Confederates and banned from coming back and responded to those who protested this First Amendment violation, "Must I shoot a simple-minded soldier boy who deserts while I must not touch a hair of a wily agitator who induces him to desert?"

Vallandigham eventually made his way to Canada, announced there his candidacy for the governorship of Ohio, lost at the polls, and was soon largely forgotten. But his views impelled some people to action, and today the wily atheist who leads simple-headed young men and women to believe that there is no God vastly increases their likelihood of committing adultery, stealing, and breaking other commandments.

Many studies now show that religious belief and church attendance reduce the likelihood of unmarried pregnancy, crime, and many other negatives. Even Bill Clinton asked, "Don't you believe that if every kid in every difficult neighborhood in America were in a religious institution on weekends . . . don't you really believe that the drug rate, the crime rate, the violence rate, the sense of self-destruction would go way down and the quality and character of this country would go way up?"

The Bible shows that God hates both actions that assume His absence and the advocacy of those actions, and not only because of their consequences: The atheist also offends God directly. This does not mean that we should forcefully silence agitators; God has said, "Vengeance is mine." Nor does it mean that atheists should be deprived of speech in contemporary America. Nor does it mean that we should assume God is taking vengeance when a disaster occurs. Sudden death, like benevolent rainfall, falls on both the just and the unjust.

God knows, and we suppose—often incorrectly. My own hope is that God shows mercy much more often than vengeance. Christians should be particularly grateful that through God's greatest mercy, Christ's sacrifice, our sins are covered over, or else we would deserve vengeance. But if God were to exile the wily atheist, would that be unfair?

STANDING FOR CHRIST WITHOUT BECOMING DEPRESSED

The good news is that God is greater than even the greatest president, but He still has an open office door, not one guarded by the Secret Service. This cannot be emphasized enough: Christianity is different from other religions not only in its theological propositions, but also in its offer of a father-son relationship with God, rather than the master-slave view of Islam or the bargaining relationship of other religions.

Sons cannot be neutral in regard to their fathers and generally regard them highly at first. Some fathers are rogues, but sin can make teenagers rebel against even good fathers and be blind to how much they owe them. Children's feelings may stay confused for a time, but maturity begins when they stop trusting their phantasms and start following the Bible by honoring fathers and mothers.

One other danger is that, because of sin, some Christians fall back into a command-and-control pattern of thinking about God or start emphasizing works rather than grace. Christians in practice often fail, but Christianity does not intrinsically require a bait-and-switch like Marxism, Eastern religions, Islam, and other faiths. Marxism, since it opposes market systems in which people freely choose among products and services, must turn dictatorial. The Buddhist resolve not to become attached to anything must include not becoming attached to people. Islam has lived with the sword and made its opponents die by the sword.

God, though, offered and offers a familial relationship that continues, as the Bible notes almost at its end, in chapter 21 of the book of Revelation: "They will be his people, and God himself will be with them as their God. He will wipe away every tear from their eyes, and death shall be no more, neither shall there be mourning nor crying nor pain" (vv. 3-4 ESV). And in the meantime, how do we live as we stand for Christ? Through confidence in the gospel and through avoiding rage by trusting in God's sovereignty.

"I have calmed and quieted my soul," the poet-king David tells us in Psalm 131:2 ESV, "like a weaned child with its mother; like a weaned child is my soul within me." That's good advice for Christians in America today. Lots of things can anger us, but few apparitions are uglier and less useful than a red-faced, vein-popping, clamor-voiced defender of a religion that emphasizes loving our neighbors. Christ sometimes was angry but always showed the self-control of one who knew the Father is in control.

If I were not slowly learning, at nearly fifty-three years of age, half of them as a Christian, to calm and quiet my soul, I'd be irate that in August 2002 the mayor of Portland declared a "Leather Pride Week" for her city. This was not an occasion for selling more handbags and shoes, but an extension of "Gay Pride" events toward frontiers of perverse sexual activity. When the culturally left *Village Voice* ran an article praising a New York City sadomasochistic event, the author noted that "every other guy was decorated with a sash bearing his title—International Drummerboy, Mr. Baltimore Eagle, American Leatherman, International Mr. Deaf Leather, to name just a few—which provided many opportunities for genuflecting." Rather than screaming at those who genuflect to false gods, we should pity them and pray for them.

How did the apostle Paul maintain his sanity and lower his blood pressure when he walked around Athens, seeing idols on every corner and shrine prostitutes at many temples? How did Daniel participate in the government of Babylon? They calmed and quieted their souls, and I suspect they also saw the humor in some of the religions their neighbors professed.

For example, what should we make of a press release headlined, "Who Knew Chickens Could Be So Endearing? Three Chickens' Rights Groups Urge Media to Do Positive Stories"? Here's the lead:

"Three U.S. animal rights organizations are urging the news media to balance chicken industry advertising with positive stories about chickens during National Chicken Month." I thought at first this was a hoax, but the press release was only the latest in a series that included one proclaiming, "Frank Perdue Now Available as a Voodoo Doll." It was true, as the press release noted, that celebrated *New York Times* writer William Grimes published a book in 2002, *My Fine-Feathered Friend*, that details Grimes's "strong emotional attachment to a chicken."

How should we react in a strange land where unborn children are killed while a battle rages over whether to eat chicken? How did Daniel react when King Belshazzar of Babylonia put on a flowing feast for 1,000 of his closest friends and desecrated golden goblets taken from the destroyed temple in Jerusalem? As the king with his nobles, wives, and concubines got drunk "and praised the gods of gold and silver, bronze, iron, wood, and stone," Daniel calmly praised the God of the Bible and interpreted for the mocking crowd the writing on the wall: "God has numbered the days of your kingdom and brought it to an end" (Dan. 5:26 ESV).

Has God numbered the days of our American liberty theme park? Is He bringing them to an end? If that is His will, that will be good, but I hope that God is merciful so that the end does not come anytime soon. I love singing the national anthem at baseball and football games and was even misty-eyed on July 4, 2002, at Turner Field in Atlanta, singing at the end of fireworks following the Braves' game, "I gladly stand up, next to you, and defend her still today, 'cause there ain't no doubt I love this land. God bless the USA."

Is Lee Greenwood's "God Bless the U.S.A." a bit maudlin? Yes, but Christians who sing it and live it are following God's command through Jeremiah quoted at the beginning of this book and worth quoting again at its conclusion: "Seek the welfare of the city where I have sent you into exile, and pray to the LORD on its behalf, for in its welfare you will find your welfare" (29:7 ESV). God eventually brought Israel out of the Babylonian exile according to His timing. In one sense God's people in America are in exile here, waiting for the new heaven and new earth that God will supply according to His timing. But as we wait, we can enjoy God's blessings, including the blessing of liberty that allows us to worship and work freely and to stand up for Christ without fearing having anything worse than rotten tomatoes hurled at us.

Enjoying that liberty and using it properly, thankful for God's grace and ready to tell others about it, we can calm and quiet our souls as we stand for Christ.

AFTERWORD

Christians with a little training can enter confidently into discussions with secular journalists because God can and might pull any journalist out of a destructive mind-set. Exhibit A could be . . . me. I grew up Jewish in New England, a regular attender of Orthodox and then Conservative synagogues, and three afternoons-a-week Hebrew schools, until age fourteen. The rabbis and teachers had wisdom, but I—with teenaged arrogance amplified by 1960s craziness—thought my brain was better. From 1965 to 1971, in high school in the Boston area and at Yale University, I saw myself as an atheist and kept moving left politically, toward what seemed intellectually cool—all the while talking a high-minded game about fighting war and poverty.

Should I scorn reporters today who sneer at conservatives or Christians and parrot what is politically correct? No, that was I three decades ago, except that I went further than most, whether it was in bicycling across the United States in 1971 or joining the unfashionable Communist Party USA in 1972. That's when I learned firsthand about the blinders that journalists may wear. Lumbering across the Pacific on a Soviet freighter, I ignored the sailors' hints about how bad things were. Training across the Soviet Union on the Trans-Siberian Railway, I ignored repression. Working at the *Boston Globe* in 1973 and writing about capitalist oppression of Portuguese immigrants, I ignored their view of America as a land of opportunity.

Given the recent decline of international communism, it's

strange to remember that thirty years ago the Soviet Union was on a roll, and the United States, enmeshed in Watergate and giving up on Vietnam, seemed helpless. In the fall of 1973, I entered graduate school at the University of Michigan, offering party-line theorizing that delighted several of my professors. Not only had I faith in socialist things unseen, but party leaders boasted of how their network of contacts would grease the way for my academic career.

That faith in socialism proved too weak. One day near the end of 1973, I was reading Lenin's famous essay "Socialism and Religion," in which he wrote, "We must combat religion—this is the ABC of all materialism, and consequently Marxism." At that point, for whatever reason, I began thinking, *What if Lenin is wrong? Why am I cutting myself off from God and all that is good?* I could not shake that thought and could no longer enthusiastically embrace communism; so I resigned from the party, thinking I was leaving the side that would eventually win.

For the next two and a half years, still at the University of Michigan graduate school, I wandered down tunnels. Having tried and abandoned liberalism and Marxism, the two dominant worldviews within the social sciences and humanities areas, there seemed nowhere else to go but into existentialism and nihilism, both of which led merely to dark rooms with more closed doors. The readings professors assigned, the magazines that received shelf space in libraries and in college bookstores, the theories that buzzed through class discussions were echoes of what I had rejected. I didn't know what else existed, but, oddly enough, while going about my business, a world of light began to appear.

Since gaining a Ph.D. required a good reading knowledge of a foreign language, in 1974 I was working to improve a poor understanding of Russian. One evening, searching my bookshelves for something in Russian I had not read, a copy of the New Testament in Russian (given to me two years before as a novelty item/joke) turned up. I began reading just for practice and kept reading because, to my surprise, the words had the ring of truth. (It helped that I had to read very slowly.)

Since graduate students taught courses to pay the bills, I had to teach a course each term. My assignment in 1975 was to teach colonial American literature, largely made up of sermons by Jonathan Edwards and other Puritan preachers. The intellect of those dead white males impressed me; I could no longer sneer at Christianity as many journalists still do, calling it a religion only for the poorly educated. Later the writings of C. S. Lewis and Francis Schaeffer showed me that Christian hearts and brains could coexist in the twentieth century as well.

In short, I was not a searcher; I was a runner, still not paying much attention to first things, still busying myself with the chores and snores in front of me. Victorian poet Francis Thompson's *The Hound of Heaven* tells the story of many conversions, including my own: "I fled him, down the nights and down the days. I fled him, down the arches of the years . . ." And yet, "with unhurrying chase, and unperturbed pace," Christ pursued—and that can give us comfort as we talk with apparently unmovable journalists.

Soon after receiving a Ph.D., I became something far more important: a follower of Christ. I visited a church picked out of the yellow pages and heard more of the gospel. After two months an old deacon of visitation came to visit at my apartment. We didn't have an intellectual discussion. He said, referring to the teaching at church, "You believe this stuff, right?" I said yes. He said, "Then you'd better sign up." I agreed, was baptized, and joined the church.

My inconsistency during the decade leading up to that change was extreme. Some people by force of habit stay in one pattern all their lives, but my own record through age twenty-six was so spotty that I know it has not been by my own power that I've been consistent in belief and action since then. While living within a culture that emphasizes doing what feels right moment by moment, I've been faithfully married for twenty-seven years and able to do a decent job raising four children. Not by my own power, since I am prone to wander, have I worked at the DuPont Company and (for two decades) at the University of Texas. Not by my own power, since I am by nature inhospitable, have I sometimes been able to act compassionately.

A profession of faith may occur many times, like quitting smoking; so the evidence of how God has changed a life is more telling. My prayer life still needs gearing up, and some sinful thoughts remain. But that I'm able to proceed at all as a husband, father, writer, professor, editor of *World*, and elder of Redeemer Presbyterian Church is a tribute to God, not to myself, because all my instincts left me facing closed doors in dark corridors. I could not even have prayed for God to be as kind to me as He has, because I had no understanding of what to pray for.

Thanks be to God.

New Year's Day, 2003

INDEX